W9-COJ-023

Literary Property

Books by RICHARD WINCOR

Literary Property

Richard Wincor

Elizabeth Seton College Library
Yonkers, New York

Clarkson N. Potter, Inc./Publisher NEW YORK

DISTRIBUTED BY CROWN PUBLISHERS, INC.

658.91
W 762

For M

COPYRIGHT © 1967, BY RICHARD WINCOR
LIBRARY OF CONGRESS CATALOG CARD NUMBER: 67-16524
ALL RIGHTS RESERVED
MANUFACTURED IN THE UNITED STATES OF AMERICA
FIRST EDITION

CONTENTS

INTRODUCTION

Writing as property, and its uses in major communications industries, are subjects that have been curiously neglected at a time when there are treatises on everything from acupuncture to Zen. One reason is prudence, since anyone who describes existing customs runs into the anthropologist's problem: he says Midsummer Eve is a bank holiday in Gotland, and somebody else says it isn't. Documentation is not always available to show who errs.

Nevertheless the potency of the recorded word is so awesome, and arrangements for its ownership are so intricate, that a textbook on rights dealing is long overdue. Producers and writers, literary agents and lawyers are some of the people concerned daily with this baffling subject. The stakes are high. A script sale may shape destiny by what it brings to an audience. Short of that it will almost certainly affect the fortunes of those on each side of the resultant contract. Still there are no textbooks on Writing As A Major Industry, only books on Copyright, which deal with legal aspects of the field. A copyright book is easier to write because there is plenty of learned authority to cite in footnotes. In preparing *From Ritual to Royalties* several years ago I found this to be true; there was always a law case, or a statute or monograph that could be rung in for support of a position. But with major film sales and television series contracts one learns quickly that cases and monographs are nothing but scenery. What lawyers call trade custom really governs transactions concerning literary property. Trade custom in turn finds its way into private contracts which are locked up in files and may not ordinarily be disclosed by those to whom they were entrusted in confidence.

My examples in most cases omit names and in all cases disguise the relationship between names and the particulars of contracts. I can assure the reader, however, that the examples and patterns in this book reflect true events. Where something unusual is exemplified to make royalty computations come out even, or to show what happens occasionally with writers of the top rank, I have indicated this to be so. It is important to remember that actual figures and prices quoted are examples only, negotiable in every instance and never standard. We shall be examining patterns, not rules.

One further point ought to be made before the traditional acknowledgment to my peers, and that is the difficulty of keeping up to the minute in a dynamic and changing industry. As this is being written the dramatic "special" on videotape has undergone a renaissance in television. Costly "pilot" films are being partly replaced by short presentation segments. New American copyright legislation is afoot. While the outcome of these and other business and legal developments is uncertain, the patterns in this book are unlikely to change fundamentally. Tomorrow's headlines in the theatre and book sections always come down to new formulations of classic formulas. The hardware changes, but literary property rules are less easily upset by new inventions. They were devised with too great difficulty to admit of complete revolution.

These developments are of interest mainly to specialists, but one somber and dramatic event at Christmas of 1966 captured the imagination of the world at large. I mean, of course, the headline dispute over William Manchester's book, *The Death of a President*, resulting in a suit by Mrs. John F. Kennedy against the author and his publishers, Harper &

Row and *Look Magazine*. Repercussions extended as far as Taiwan, where book pirates often make a practice of publishing unauthorized editions, and West Germany, The Netherlands and Denmark, where publishers asserted their right to serialize the unauthorized edition. There may never have been a literary case either so well publicized or so tragically disturbing.

Straight off I should say that the known record supports Mrs. Kennedy. Still, nothing in this world is simple, leaving aside the presumptuous question whether the late President's family were well advised at every step of the way. Surely the famous "Memorandum of Understanding" could have been drafted more carefully. Its key paragraph as reported in *The New York Times* provides, "The completed manuscript shall be reviewed by Mrs. John F. Kennedy and Robert F. Kennedy, and the text shall not be published unless and until approved by them." The first part of this paragraph—"shall be reviewed"—suggests an affirmative obligation which was unnecessary and potentially dangerous even when read together with later provisions appointing Edward F. Kennedy or his designee as alternates for the giving of approval. It would have been better to say merely that no publication would be authorized without approval. More specific machinery for indicating approval coupled with prearranged payment by those withholding it are not unknown in trade custom and might have forestalled this poignant controversy. Some of the telegrams in the case similarly appear a trifle cryptic but, of course, there were other factors as well, which are undisclosed.

Nevertheless Senator Kennedy did have a contract calling for approval of text and of subsidiary rights sales, with a restriction against publishing before November 22, 1968. If, thereby, he tied the publishers in knots, that was his privilege under his agreement. Without proof of his alleged consent to change the ground rules, the publisher's statements about history appear wide of the mark. The real issue was not history versus privacy, but what the parties had agreed.

In this book I have emphasized the careful wording of contracts and dealt with subjects that have a familiar ring as one considers the Manchester book case. One of these subjects is ownership of secrets. Another is inspection of underlying rights documents when somebody warrants he has everything you need in the way of clearance. Still another is script approval. Nothing about *The Death of a President* made me want to recall my manuscript from the printer and alter the text. What I do regret is that my special subject has been catapulted into the news in circumstances that caused anguish. There are not even any villains in this cast. The whole affair is really a dramatic illustration of a dry point: the value of professionalism.

I am indebted to Messrs. Salvatore J. Iannucci, Jr., Harold S. Klein, Robert H. Montgomery, Jr., Clarkson N. Potter, Paul R. Reynolds, Jr., and Harold H. Stern (listed alphabetically) for looking over portions of the text and making useful suggestions before it went to the printer. Final responsibility for everything in the book, however, including any errors, is solely my own. I am also grateful to Miss Leslie J. Wiggin for her admirable typing and most of all to my wife, who offered many helpful suggestions including the modification of several passages that sounded even more acerb than I had intended when I wrote them.

Literary property is one of the hard subjects like Latin, but worth doing. While rushing in where agents fear to tread, I am reminded of some famous lines from *Paradise Lost, II*:

> A gulf profound as that Serbonian bog
> Betwixt Damiata and Mount Casius old,
> Where armies whole have sunk.

However suitable, the quoted passage has one prime virtue, namely, that Milton is not under copyright, and requires no clearance. That virtue is lacking in the kinds of property we shall consider in this book. They are not in the public domain. Somebody owns them, or parts of them, and somebody else wants particular rights to fashion them into a book or a play, a motion picture or a television series. What then occurs is the subject of our book.

I have appended a short glossary of industry terms which may prove useful in a field where technical vocabulary is inescapable.

RICHARD WINCOR

New York City
March, 1967

BASIC ELEMENTS

As WRITING IS ONE OF THE DESPERATE PROFESSIONS, IT has universal appeal, especially for those who are not engaged in it. Writing as an art has its own literature; writing as a major industry is largely undocumented. There are no jungle maps, only some good copyright treatises and collections of annotated form contracts.

In this book I have tried sketching basic patterns that recur in dealing with literary property. At best it can be only a beginning; each medium such as television and the legitimate theatre has its own ground rules, and nobody can know all of them. Then too, practice differs in the three principal markets most likely to serve as processing stations before literary material reaches an English-speaking audience.

London is a market for books, plays and films—actually all forms of recorded communication. Still the practice until recently has been to make simple and direct arrangements. Producers and agents write down the main points, such as money, and exchange copies of relatively simple documents rather than sign the same contract page. Something less than every conceivable possibility is spelled out. What happens if Australia wants to buy television rights to the main character of a play based on a novel is not always anticipated. There are signs, however, that the more complex American pattern is becoming more familiar, and the position may change.

A second communications center is the Los Angeles

area, or "West Coast." Here the film industry has shaped custom, and as a result most transactions concerning literary rights are highly technical. Contracts go on and on about copyright. Arrangements generally are formal, meticulous and perhaps not very imaginative. Management tries for outright script ownership. The reasons are self-evident since relatively few feature films are produced, and usually at high cost. The same atmosphere characterizes West Coast television production, although in this medium the writer often receives lower pay and has a better chance that some of his rights will eventually be returned to him.

The New York or "East Coast" school is something different again. As in London, all of the communications media flourish. Playwrights and novelists arrange most of their American transactions in this area since theatres and publishing houses are grouped here. Many film company decisions are eastern but reflect West Coast practice. In television, which is more flexible, the live or videotape dramatic and comedy-variety program has left its mark. The East Coast approach is generally flexible, informal and more likely than not "pro-author." An important part of the game is anticipating how writings go from one medium to another. A story may become a Broadway musical, and its characters may be extracted for use in television.

This book in the main reflects the East Coast approach.

Two other subjects require mention before literary rights dealings are outlined. One is the nature of the creative process itself; the other is law and its relation to recorded communications.

Nobody can write authoritatively of the creative process. It is a mystery. Yet some of the various theories concerning its nature are worth mulling.

First, in accordance with fashion, is the "scientific approach." Man has more cerebrum than monkeys do. Mozart's *Jupiter Symphony* can be explained by the interaction of neural blocks, reflexes and motor pathways as affected by chemicals and drugs. R. W. Gerard's essay, "The Biological Basis of Imagination," follows these lines.

A second approach is based on the notion of unconscious borrowing. Writing is a fusion of what others have done or said. The classic study here is *The Road to Xanadu* by John Livingston Lowes. In this treatise Professor Lowes traces the sources of Coleridge's imagination to a number of interesting places, ranging from Abyssinia to the British Museum. "Those caves of ice" in *Kubla Khan* are the result of "interfusion."

A third theory attracts followers of Plato. Reality is a world of forms or ideas; what we perceive here is a mere copy. Very likely a Neoplatonist would consider Tony Weller more real than Dickens. C. E. M. Joad puts it well in a discussion of infant prodigies:

I like to think that one of the reasons for it may be that the soul has inhabited such an order of reality before it was incarnated in the body, and brings with it to this world a memory of the harmonies of sound and combinations of number which exist in that world, a memory which it does not immediately forget.

A fourth notion is held by the Tibetan lamas. There are fictitious beings called "tulpas" who come into existence through somebody's intense concentration, and dissolve similarly if they do not get out of hand. Being projections of the creator's subconscious, they can become pretty difficult at awkward times. Alexandra David-Neel, a Frenchwoman who "created" one, complained that it followed her caravan through Tibet and that others could see it. So psychological and occult an approach might explain fictional characters and the spells they cast over the public mind.

There you have four theories about the creative process. Perhaps all of them are partially true; the point is that literature is different from other property. By its nature it defies boundaries and blurs price tags.

Many of these difficulties are reflected in the laws concerning literary property. The French, for example, never have accepted somebody's writing as simple property. French law conceives it as a projection of the author's personality and protects it against tampering under a doctrine called *droit moral*—the moral right. American film companies naturally loathe such a concept since it inhibits making script changes without the author's consent.

News just off the wire further illustrates how hard it is to force something incorporeal into a legal frame. The Supreme Court of the United States has held news—not a copyrighted dispatch but the information itself, before general disclosure—to be "quasi-property." A great many articles on copyright law take similar refuge from the English language where there are no words that fit. Latin is a perennial favorite, but German is becoming modish again.

Obviously a play or novel is something special; one is tempted to say *sui generis*, or its German equivalent. Nevertheless it is property of a sort, being susceptible of ownership and distinct from the physical copy recording it.

Works of literature are a bizarre form of property. They cannot be owned forever except in the case of certain university copyrights in England protected by special statutes. Their component words are in the public domain, leaving only specific word sequences and sometimes concepts as well under legal protection. Questions of time and space arise as they do not with other kinds of property, such as land or hardware. For how long do I own my book or script? How much of it do I ever own? These are the legal questions that arise.

Copyright is the traditional doctrine that protects literature. Publish some sort of recorded communication in any medium and you can secure copyright for a fixed term of years, provided you comply with certain formalities. National laws differ, but international treaties and conventions conduce harmony. Copyright protects the owner against substantial

copying of his work. There is no fixed number of lines that
can be used without permission, and it is not easy to predict
what a court will consider piracy. Copyright also protects
compilations and derivative works. A Dutch translation of
a musical based on *Cymbeline* is a separate right, but only
the new matter is protected. *Cymbeline* remains in the public
domain; somebody else can set it to music, or do a Dutch
version, or both. If he does so, of course, he must either hire
his own composer and Dutch translator or clear rights in the
first Dutch version or musical.

Copyright is so closely connected with literary property
that often the two are made synonymous. This equation, however, is a mistake; stranger elements are involved. The distinction between copyright infringement and less direct invasion
of literary rights is best illustrated by a glance at both ex-
tremes.

Consider first a classic infringement of copyright. Let us
assume that the B.B.C. is broadcasting a new play on television. I do two things: I set up a pirate broadcasting station
outside United Kingdom territorial waters, and I run off
thousands of paperback copies of the play. These are straight
copyright infringements. One or more actions lie against me,
not to mention the likelihood of my being unwelcome for a
time in London broadcasting and publishing circles.

Consider, however, something rather more subtle. Somebody does a television series dominated by mention of a
character who never appears, like Quint in "The Innocents."
Just this device was used for a time on Australian television—
no ghost, but a fictitious woman called Mavis Bramston—
until viewers required that she appear as a running part in
the series. Suppose I had done three things: (1) put on a
similar series about an absent woman called Prunella, or
(2) the same, actually calling her Mavis, or (3) the same as
(2) but with Mavis appearing on camera throughout the
series. Traditionalists might say there are no legal problems
here. I am not so sure—whichever bit of borrowing you select.

Turning to grander outrages along the same line, assume that this isolated passage appears in a book about spy systems:

Aged Dr. Jelinek, Headmaster of the dreaded Danube Academy for Mine-Sowing and Espionage (DAME), winked his one eye and rapped for order with the celebrated Nairobi Sword Cane that had figured so prominently in the recent Affair of the Soviet Field Marshal.
"Give the password, boys," croaked Dr. Jelinek.
"Neatness at all times," replied the boys in unison.

It is easy to see a television series growing out of this fragment, but suppose I (1) actually sell a series with all this in it, or (2) same, but change Jelinek's name, give him the more usual number of eyes, and invent a new password, or (3) do one of these things after the author has his own series on television featuring DAME. Traditionalists would say the first two possibilities are not a problem since we are dealing with mere ideas. This is questionable, but certainly (3) can mean trouble. The reason is that a running series of identifying devices—the Headmaster, his school and various recurring props or effects—have become established with the public, identifying the one creative source and coming very much to life. In effect, they are trademarks.

Now trademarks (including titles, which cannot be copyrighted) have their own system of legal protection. Once distinctive, or having acquired "secondary meaning," their dominant features are protected by the law of unfair competition. Another case of quasi-property and some new muddles.

These distinctions are not merely theoretical. If you have a right to prevent someone from stealing your best characters, or a fictitious school, does it follow that these elements are separate properties independent of the original copyrighted text in which they appeared? If extracted and transplanted, they may create new sources of income. The transplants themselves are not quite copyrights, not quite trademarks. I suggest they constitute new forms of property.

If this is so, there are going to be problems in dealing with these elements for years to come. How long can you "own" a fictitious locale? Can you assign rights in your original race of beings from Jupiter? Can you put into your will the great Battle of Martha's Vineyard, which never really occurred? Copyright rules are no use here. The Supreme Court of the United States has indicated hostility to expanding existing protection by going round by the side door. Still the new forms of property will not go away. Sherlock Holmes is something more than a collection of specific tales. He *exists*.

Two rather different law principles deserve mention at this point. They can be thought of as obligations, not rights. One is an inherent right to be afforded proper name or "billing" credit for authorship, and its converse is the right not to have one's work attributed to the wrong author. A second obligation is to avoid naming live people without their written permission, and to avoid defaming them by wrongful identification whether they are named or not. These doctrines are respectively called right of privacy and libel or slander. They deserve careful consideration in dealing with literary property.

One illustration from actual practice should suffice. I once spent all morning with the production staff and writer of a prospective television program about a recent military operation. The problem was one of the officers who had been in on it. He had got wind of our show plan and had written threatening letters explaining that his true role in the affair was a property right which he preferred selling elsewhere. Our job, then, was to purge the script of all reference to him. This officer was never named in the script but he kept popping up in all sorts of bad places where only he could have been present in true life. Scene after scene came out, to the writer's dismay. Finally there was one scene that absolutely could not be deleted. Without it the whole script would collapse. Yet there he was, planning Operation X, as he had done in the real campaign. Somebody on the production staff found an ingenious solution: the character was changed into a female officer. She appeared in the one scene, planned Operation X and disappeared from the story. Our threatening friend never was heard from again. He would really have been on the spot if he said that the lady was he; exit mincingly.

These are some of the legal questions that come up in connection with writing. Most of them concern ownership, several others, the avoidance of liability. Dividing rights and responsibilities in both areas is part of dealing with literary property. Neither my outline of applicable law nor the preceding notes on the creative process is complete. I have sketched them only as background. Legal problems must be put to lawyers; sources of the creative process may be a question for philosophers.

Summing up:

Literary property in the English language is likely sooner or later to be processed in one or more of three principal communications capitals.

The approach in this book is primarily that of the American East Coast school.

Sources of the creative process are the subject of disagreement.

Laws applicable to literary property are not precision instruments.

Copyright goes just so far and then you have to worry about new forms of literary property.

You must be careful what you say.

The division of rights and the apportionment of risks are the essence of dealing in recorded communications—books, plays, videotape specials, film series and other products of creative imagination.

There is a thicket of abstractions to work through, before you come to the inn.

At this stage it may be useful to consider some of the

main elements. There is a traditional cast of characters who deal regularly in literary property, and they can be divided into two teams: the Owners and the Users.

The Owners (it might be simpler calling them Authors, but not every writer retains ownership of his work, and not every literary rights owner actually creates what he sells) control incorporeal property which they are putting up for sale. I use "sale" in the lay sense, meaning sale, license or other disposition of rights. Nobody wants to grant all prospective rights if he can keep some of them. Usually, one grants rights for some specific use or series of uses which the buyer needs for his own purposes.

On the other side are the Users. It seems best to eschew any temptation to put money labels on what they actually do. They could be called buyers, but as often as not they are something less than that, merely licensees—people or companies granted the equivalent of easements or mineral rights on another's estate. Generally what the Users pay for is the right but not the obligation to use literary material. They do not have to put on a man's play. They can merely pay him the agreed minimum within the time limits prescribed.

The Owner is frequently an author represented by a literary agent and a copyright lawyer. Sometimes an accountant comes in to advise with respect to tax planning in a particular transaction. There are times when the author's publisher acts as his agent for the sale of other rights. Some of the agencies in turn purport to offer the author free legal counsel as an additional service. Lawyers have been known to act as agents, and union or guilds representing writers not infrequently have a try at all of these roles. Generally the author gets the service he pays for. As with everything else, there are no bargains.

The Owner may very well be a large corporation or partnership. A firm of this sort may own outright particular scripts it has commissioned, or own by assignment a library of film copyrights which it puts on the market. Many of the larger companies negotiate through staff counsel. Then too, the Owner may be the estate of a deceased author, or a trust, or a hospital, as with some of the rights in *Peter Pan*. Determining who owns what rights is essential.

The User is generally a production company, distributor, publisher, network or station, advertising agency or limited partnership, that is to say, one of the formal and continuing business entities that traffic in literary material. Generally they negotiate through counsel, not agents. Agents are for selling, and the Users are buying. Not all of them, though, are big houses. Sometimes a star performer buys rights in a script as a vehicle in which to appear. Directors may buy something to direct, composers buy scripts to adapt as musicals. Still, in many of these cases the rights eventually are "laid off" on or assigned to one of the traditional large companies that act as Users. What was originally paid probably will be recouped in the second sale.

Another category of Users is educational institutions, ranging from schools to libraries. What they have in common is a dislike of paying for what they use. Their proposals for free use of other people's literary property has been a subject of brisk dispute in American copyright legislation.

The Owners and the Users play out a complex game with bizarre rules. They carry on a vast dialogue founded on basic themes. File after file closes, books run their course, series come to an end, the vast dialogue goes on.

This is a list of the subjects most frequently negotiated in all media, the positions generally taken by each side and some typical resolutions in final contract.

The User wants warranties of title so as to know the nature of the rights he is acquiring. The safest thing he can do is to have his attorney order a copyright search from a professional service and to insist on inspection of underlying rights documents in the chain of title. Thereafter, to be on the safe side, he will still want to hang all of the risk on the Owner. The risk might be anything from libel in the material itself to the possibility that the same script has been previously sold to somebody else or so encumbered as to be useless. Frequently the Owner's warranties mean very little unless the Owner is solvent (which most authors are not) and so it becomes necessary to request guarantees by some entity standing behind the Owner—if one exists. You are not very likely to get this with writers but you may find it useful when buying from small companies that distribute through larger ones.

Usually, the Owner is not too happy about taking on all of the risk. Often he seeks to confine his liability to the amount he receives under the contract with his User, for example, the amount of his fee or royalties. With more justice he demands cross-indemnification from his User with respect to literary material that the User interpolates in the final production, if the User has that right at all under their contract. Similarly, if the User's attorney has had the chance to inspect any underlying rights documents, all the Owner may choose to warrant is that these are true copies of all known applicable papers evidencing title, since the User can draw his own conclusions from what he reads.

A typical compromise might confine the Owner's liability, in the event his warranties prove untrue, to an amount double his share under the contract. In this way he is made to bear some of the risk but is spared complete ruin. Typically, any User will cross-indemnify as to his own interpolations, but guarantees by ultimate Users are not typical at all. In cases where the material is especially risky, both sides may make a run on Lloyds and negotiate a division of premiums if insurance comes in.

Warranties and indemnities are more than techniques, they are a frame of mind. Essentially they reflect disbelief that the Owner can grant what he is supposed to grant, and forebodings about the consequences of producing his play or publishing his manuscript. This is a legalistic approach, and a good one if carried off gracefully. Without it you may be buying the exclusive rights to use Westminster Abbey or something equally as evanescent in script material.

So extended an apology for surly pragmatism may fittingly conclude with an illustration. I once was asked who owned ad-libs uttered by spacemen in orbit. In answering this as best I could, I put questions of my own about who bore the risk if the ad-libs were published without permission. It was this latter point that usurped the discussion. Nobody wants to infringe copyrights but sometimes the law itself is uncertain. In such cases laying off risk is ultimately the real problem. My recommendation, naturally, was that someone else bear this risk. In this way, an intriguing copyright speculation turned into the formulation of a practical plan delineating areas of responsibility.

Putting somebody else on the hook is distasteful idiom but standard procedure. Any agreement skirting the question of division of risk must be considered overly sanguine. Any script may turn out to have been pirated, or filled with libel, or encumbered by conflicting grants to others. When these things happen, somebody pays the piper. Better business practice dictates that the victim be marked in advance.

The nature of rights granted is a question concerning time and space in the broadest sense: time in that the User wants rights for the longest possible time and the Owner wants cut-off rights so that he may choose better later on; space in that the User wants world rights in all media while the Owner prefers letting go as little as possible for the price, for example, one telecast in Japan only, and without pay television, community antenna boosters and all that. Possibly I have overstated the Owner's reluctance. He may be willing to grant more extensive rights so long as the User successfully exploits his material, but he is unlikely to find an ideal marriage.

The traditional compromise is a grant of rights in a specific medium for a fixed time in a limited territory. It may be agreed in advance that the User picks up new rights if he does well with the original ones. This sort of mixed bag is most frequently seen in the theatre; run somebody's play X performances and you get British rights or a share of film proceeds. In other media this kind of conditional mixed bag is less popular.

The rights grant very often is coupled with restrictions on rights reserved by the Owner. A play may be hurt by a film based on the same property and released simultaneously in the same city. One telecast may spoil the chance of a film sale, and so on. Therefore anyone buying limited rights had better assure himself that his rights are exclusive as far as they go, and that competing rights reserved by the Owner will not suddenly draw off his audience. A part of what Users buy is non-use by others. Playing dog in the manger is quite necessary for protection. When the rights purchased expire, then the restricted rights come unfrozen again and the Owner can use them.

The most complex rights purchases are by the producer unable to make up his mind about a particular property. Such and such a novel might make a good play, but perhaps it would do better as a film. In these circumstances he pays more for the privilege of choosing later.

"Subsidiary rights" is a key phrase here. The words mean rights in media other than the medium in which the sale is made. Thus they mean different things depending on the User's specialty. To a book publisher, film rights are subsidiaries. To a film company film rights are not subsidiaries at all. The term has no fixed reference to any one medium; it should be taken with a grain of salt, like the word "foreigner."

Something far more subtle than subsidiary rights has no name at all but can be just as important. I refer to the extricable component elements of complete literary works and their "spin-off" possibilities. A single character may be extracted from one television series and used in a new series. A text format may engender a learned quarterly. I mentioned earlier that some of these elements may be new forms of property. Whatever they are—if they are anything valuable—they ought to be carved up and divided by contract.

All of the rights mentioned are generally taken under option rather than purchased outright. By "option," I mean the right to choose within a prearranged time period whether or not to go forward with a project. For a payment smaller than the ultimate purchase price the User hedges his bet, using the option period to see whether he can raise money, engage the right cast and do all of the other things essential to exploit the material. The clock ticks out on him; so many months for so much, so many months more for additional payments or advances against royalties, and finally the last option to go all the way with his rights or lose them. Options buy time and lessen the risk of investment. Once in a great while Users agree to pay damages for failure on their part to produce or publish. Failure to exercise a last option, however, usually results in nothing more than loss of all rights. The Owner keeps what he has received so far and looks for another producer or publisher.

Sometimes even an option may be more than the Owner will grant or the User will pay for. In these cases one often negotiates a right of first refusal or first negotiation. Variously defined in individual contracts, these lesser-than-option rights follow a fixed pattern. The burdensome right of first refusal is the right to meet the terms of a competing offer within an agreed time period; "meeting the terms" should be spelled out because, while the User might be able to match his rival's offer dollar for dollar, he might not be able to cast the same star as the lead, or rent the same theatre. The right of first negotiation in turn is almost no right at all. It amounts to your having to talk first to somebody before offering a work to others. First refusals and first negotiations may be used in a number of instances, for example, with an author's next book, or his next book on a particular subject or character.

All too often these terms are used imprecisely. We hear

that a play is sold when actually it is under option. We are told somebody has an option when he has nothing at all, or nothing that can be enforced. The distinctions are meaningful and worth taking a little trouble to maintain.

A frequent adjunct to rights is the acquisition of the author's services. Services and rights tend to get mixed up, and it takes close attention to keep the two straight. None of it is as easy as it sounds.

Services involve unions and guilds. Unions in turn usually mean minimum scale payments, requirements as to billing credit, residuals, pension and welfare contributions and other such protections. One of the most important safeguards for writers is the enforced time limit on holding rights, even if the User is willing to pay more for an extension. The notion is that nobody should be able to immobilize a writer's work indefinitely just by making minimal option payments from time to time. There comes a point when the User must do something more or stand aside.

It follows that Users may be better off buying rights as such, not services. If adaptations are needed they can put their own staff people on the job, often as not writers better qualified than the author. Sometimes union contracts for services are avoided by putting somebody in as "Production Consultant" even though he contributes literary material. This device is not necessarily dishonest; creative functions tend to spill over into one another, and who actually is the author in a creative process is a question for Aquinas.

Collective bargaining agreements change every few years and are scarcely appropriate for detailed treatment in a book on property rights. The point worth remembering is that every time an author is employed to do more work in getting his property ready for public presentation, a collective bargaining agreement may have to be referred to.

Not all writers' organizations are true unions. Some guide and lobby for their membership, for example, the Authors' Guild in the book field. Others go beyond this and insist on substantial adherence to their form contracts even without union status and without "employee" members. The Dramatists' Guild, which governs acquisition of plays in the legitimate theatre, is the example here. Finally there are the real writers' unions such as the Writers' Guild of America, Inc. which has done much to shape business practice in television and motion pictures.

In the main, going from one medium to another means no union. If I buy film rights to "McNab's" novel (the name "McNab" having a good sound to it), I can freely work out the terms with the author or his representative; but if McNab goes Hollywood and makes it a condition that he leave Buffalo and write the screenplay, I have a different problem. As against that, there will be union jurisdiction over my contract with somebody else, but I will at least have time to choose him and I start off as a partial rights owner myself.

Payment structures mean very little until people define the property changing hands, and the conditions of transfer. Payment for rights follows certain fixed patterns. Though the specific modes can become indescribably complex, especially when stock or something other than money makes up part of the price, the main lines are clear.

First, payments usually are hedged by options, i.e., not committed all at one time. Each successive payment reflects a decision to buy time.

Second, there is generally some sort of down payment on signing. Frequently this amount is a guaranteed non-returnable advance against something contingent, such as a share of profits. Whether it is or is not an advance ought to be made clear.

Third, there may be royalties or "residuals," payments computed on fixed formulas but made only if the property is used or re-used. For example, a television writer might get a royalty of $500 per new program episode for creating the main character, or a residual payment of $500 for each such episode shown in the United Kingdom a year later. Then too, there are the additional possibilities of his getting both, or neither.

Fourth, payment sometimes may be a percentage of "gross receipts," that is, everything that comes in at the box office less a few special items such as local taxes. This mode of payment is highly desirable in most cases but is standard so far only in the legitimate theatre.

Fifth and last among standard payment provisions is the share of "net profits." No concept in the field is so likely to inspire suspicion if not cynicism, and no trade term requires such elaborate definition in page after page of well justified paranoia. Net profits generally refer to the amount left after deducting all production and distribution costs, frequently including a percentage of budget allocated to reflect overhead, the shares of net profits payable to others, and other elements. In these circumstances everyone else may be paid first out of a given dollar or pound, with the net profits position very much last in line. More specifically, there are not likely to be any net profits. Even when there are, dishonest accountings and payroll padding can erase all of it.

The net profits arrangement comes in everywhere. It was designed for speculative ventures; committed costs are kept down but everyone shares if the enterprise succeeds. Many find "net profits" unhelpful on cold nights.

With phrases like "gross receipts" and "net profits," not to mention hybrids such as "gross profits," the contract definition is everything. There are no fixed meanings. When negotiators get into a wrangle about definitions, one way out of the impasse may be by reference to a distribution contract (which itself defines net profits) signed by the User, who is party to the original rights contract. This procedure ensures that all of the victims will be treated equally. Suppose, for example, that your play is to be syndicated locally on television. Your producer will offer you his standard definition of net profits which you may find shocking, but your own will be even more unacceptable to him. As against that, each of you knows that there will probably be a third party coming into the arrangement for the purpose of distributing the producer's product. In the contract between the producer and the distributor, there will almost surely be a definition of net profits as the two plan to divide them. In anticipation of this event you may at least specify that your own clause on net profits must be no less favorable than the producer's with his distributor.

Perhaps the trickiest point is defining *whose* gross or *whose* net. One must know whether his percentage is based on the totality of something such as net profits, or on someone's share of that totality. A single example suffices: assume that the same television writer who so ingeniously worked out his definition of net profits is offered 10 percent of net profits from his show. Total net profits eventually are $100,000. Now if the writer has stipulated clearly that he gets 10 percent of 100 percent of net profits, he gets $10,000. If he has been less explicit he may be entitled only to 10 percent of what the production company that engaged him is to get as its own share of net profits. If the production company previously contracted away half its net profits in exchange for initial financing, it retains only 50 percent and the writer's 10 percent is based on $50,000. Thus the writer will receive $5,000 if his percentage is based on the producer's share instead of on 100 percent. Conceivably he might be worse off still, if the producer had been forced to give up all except 10 percent of net profits to outside interests. In that case the writer would get $1,000.

These melancholy permutations suggest care in defining percentage shares. It will not suffice to talk about "a piece of the action," to cite a popular term as inelegant as it is imprecise. A great many points must be covered: whether losses on one season's programs can be carried over to next season, whether one venture can be cross-collateralized with another between the same parties—all the situations in which one show gets by and another fails.

Whatever the traditional modes of payment, they have this common feature: most of them are designed for the remote future and do not provide funds immediately.

Many of the most sophisticated literary agents are unable to see the difference between control and money. The difference, however, is vast even though they may very swiftly translate into the same thing.

I refer less to the touchy subject of "creative control," meaning the final say over the artistic elements constituting a production, than I do to the right to decide whether a property is to be sold or licensed at all, and to whom, and on what terms. Whoever holds this right (even in veto form) is in a key position.

Again, the issue here is not how many percentage points or shares somebody may hold. Sometimes a 5 percent profit sharer may be able to thwart an important film sale against the wishes of 95 percent profit sharers, if he happens to be the author.

Control over the disposition of rights frequently is left open in simple contracts. I suggest that this is a mistake, arising out of too great a fear of discussing unpleasant possibilities at a stage when the people are all friends. Especially among collaborators is this affliction rampant. Diplomacy ought to be more than simulated friendship, and should take into account that discord is the common denominator in human affairs.

In the absence of specific contract provision, the American legal rule has been that either collaborator may grant rights without the other's consent, short of destroying the value of the property (whatever that means) and subject to an obligation to divide the spoils with his demurring co-owner. The British rule makes solo ventures of this kind impossible without the co-owner's consent, however grudging. Both rules lead straight to the cliff; the point should be worked out in each instance.

If you write a book with a collaborator, the question

whether to contract with Publisher X is less simple than it appears. Publisher X may turn out to be your collaborator's nephew publishing his first book. The control point goes even deeper. X's contracts may give him control of the film rights, which he may exercise by selling them to a different uncle, who is producing his first film. Then you have questions about alterations and setting your best brainchild to music, all horrifying prospects even though you may get half of the author's share. This is the sort of thing I mean by control. It tends to get personalized, and should be agreed in advance one way or the other. With more than two owners you may even work out a voting system to resolve discord by parliament. Under one formula the outvoted co-author keeps his financial share but has the option to remove his name. This done, he can face his public and still be remunerated for his pains.

Billing credit may be as important as money. Appropriate name credit has to be worked out, with provisions for size and placement on the screen or marquee vis-a-vis others, and for advertising and promotion within the User's control.

Subtle billing problems arise in connection with derivative works, scripts based on other writings, material changed by the User but keeping generally to the original. Here accuracy is vital. "Based on a story by," "Suggested by," "Characters created by," "Presented by arrangement with," are some of the formulas much in use. Once again it may be worth repeating that the right to delete one's name unlocks many a door without yielding the treasury.

In working out billing credit you must avoid deceiving the public. Ghostwriting, for example, is under a legal cloud as deceitful. Ghost-writers nowadays are named usually as "collaborators" with the person whose work they are paid for doing. Along similar lines the FCC requires disclosure of paid plugs in television. You cannot lawfully buy air credits for subliminal advertising. All of these principles are tied in with name credits.

The right to assign rights, fully or in part, to anyone, may sound like a mere legal detail, but the point is vital. In business terms this is the User's right to lay off his contract on somebody new. In this fashion he may protect himself against risk, and for that matter (if skilled at blandishment) against failure. All he must do is find a new buyer.

Now this right is a very good thing for the User. In some cases he may anticipate availing himself of it immediately; in the theatre, for example, somebody taking a play option might need co-producing associates to raise money. Without some of the magic words in his contract with the Owner—for example a novelist—he may have to pay the Owner more money for his omission. Similarly, the Owner might relish his own right to assign so that he could hire some hack to do his writing.

This entire area has been reasonably well explored. Author-Owners rarely can assign anything but their right to receive payment. Occasionally they may employ people to write episodes, furnishing the lot as a package. The television series is a medium where this practice not infrequently occurs. In the main, however, the creator is considered unique; he may not appoint deputies.

Owners are likely to be corporations. The artist is unique but they are not. As a result, they insist on the right to assign, the right to get out completely, or lay off on others while keeping a financial interest in the outcome, or bring in associates right from the beginning. Usually they are liable only if the assignee defaults. Sometimes the restrictions are more sweeping: they may assign their rights and obligations only to named companies, or firms of a certain stature. However it comes out, the point must be covered.

These are the seven major points in dealing with literary property. Of course there are others: *force majeure* provisions that govern in circumstances beyond one's control; most favored nations clauses that protect against somebody else's coming off better, by providing in advance to inherit these extra benefits; merger language that links an adaptation with the original work so that the two become one. These and other provisions tend to recur in patterns. Nevertheless these are specialty items. They and others are best dealt with according to media, some most suitable in publishing, others in television and some only in rare circumstances. The seven major points, though, recur constantly and in most of the known media that exist as industries.

Therefore it may be useful to pause and summarize:

Warranties. The User must satisfy himself that he is getting clear rights. He may want to inspect underlying contracts if the Owner adapted somebody else's work, and take out insurance against the possibility of error.

Rights. This is the crux of the dialogue and touches a great many issues: where and for how long, in what medium, with what exclusivity and restrictions and what assurance against competitive use of reserved rights, whether subject to Users' options and Owners' reversion rights, and in what degree applicable to offshoot and new material.

Services. When this subject comes in, so usually do the guilds and unions. Traffic in literary rights may become subject to collective bargaining agreement minimum terms.

Payment. A great deal of the compensation paid for literary property is contingent, not assured. Some of the more usual forms are royalties and residuals, and percentages of somebody's share of gross or net as defined by contract.

Control. Who has the final say as to sale or license, script changes, and whatever else requires decision is separate from money questions, but may eventually determine them.

Billing Credit. The size, placement and use of names are obsessively important in this field and are subject to rules against deceiving the public.

Assignment. Everyone wants a hedge against error and some buyers deliberately speculate for resale. The question is whether the first User can be restricted and kept liable if his successors default.

These issues are basic. Others may dwarf them in specific instances, but these seven questions always return, and require answers.

Together they are the foundations of contracts. Contract law, which fills many treatises, might have been mentioned earlier in connection with copyright and the other law doctrines that shape literary property. On the other hand, contract principles are less specialized. They are the fabric of civilized commerce, and deserve separate mention.

Contracts ought to be drawn by lawyers. That suggestion makes all but a few points academic here. What remains has to do with negotiation, and its ripening into contract. On this score I point out several worries.

First, oral commitments may, under certain circumstances, be enforced as contracts. Those that may be performed within a year and sufficiently set out the arrangement between parties do not always have to be in writing, aside from the question of proof.

Second, written contracts will not always stand up if material points are left unsettled. All the "Witnesseth" and "Whereas" clauses in the lexicon may be insufficient to save a document that leaves open the price, or the option dates, or other important matters "to be agreed in good faith" later on.

Third, contracts are created by an offer and its acceptance, no matter how many intervening counterproposals find their way into the ultimate formula. Self-serving telegrams such as "I accept your offer except that residuals are to be based on original salary instead of union scale" are unlikely to create binding commitments; you cannot pick and choose favorite terms among those offered, but at some point must accept the whole parcel to achieve contract.

Needless to say, these are oversimplifications of enormously intricate doctrines. I note these particular points because they come up so often in connection with negotiations. In the last analysis the problems are legal, but it may be a good thing to remember that contracts may result from conversations or an exchange of letters if all or most of the vital provisions have been agreed. I recall with delight the printed letterhead of an agent who at some point must have been made uncomfortably aware of these principles. It read, if I remember correctly, "Nothing in this letter is intended to create any obligation on the sender or to result in contract." That sort of caption may lose deals now and then, but it keeps one out of trouble.

Contracts on literary property rarely can be as simple as people would like them to be. The subject matter itself is too subtle; works of imagination require imaginative treatment.

The patterns discussed thus far recur in all the communications industries. Each separate medium, however, has its special ground rules and problems. Of these media, television must come first. There is no better laboratory for analysis of recorded communication and its component parts. In its own way it comprises a bibliography of the entire field. It has *all* the problems, something of a distinction for so young an art.

TELEVISION

SCIENCE OUTPACING TASTE IS THE HISTORY OF TELEVISION IN a nutshell. Beyond that it seems dangerous to generalize, and today's practice is very likely to be next season's museum piece.

In the theatre, where technology is less relevant, scripts are played out on a stage largely as they were played out thousands of years ago. Proscenium and pit differences are unlikely in themselves to govern the royalties of playwrights. In television, however, the ways in which literary material is delivered to an audience may revolutionize business practice.

Within a short time networks may disappear (or just as likely, may increase in number), community antenna boosters may grow outmoded, pay-television stagnate as a near miss, free television become a first-run outlet for motion pictures, educational television turn into a major industry, home projection of store-bought recordings flourish as a new right and the Satellite loom as the grand distributor of canned laughter throughout the world. Merlin himself would shudder.

This is not to say that any of the basic business patterns will disappear. More likely than not the seven points outlined in the first chapter will continue to be the essence of the Owner-User dialogue; the difference will appear in specific subdivisions. For example, if pay or subscription television succeeds, and the home viewer pays for his program entertainment, writers may get a fraction of gross receipts until the industry has a better idea of the probable revenue a show may produce. A development of that sort would be a departure from present practice, since until now television writers have seen gross receipts only with syndication, and then only during a brief era.

Subject to these prophesies I should like to sketch briefly how the industry trafficks in literary property at the present time.

American television grew up as a branch of advertising. Occasionally it flowered into an art form, but as the number of sets in use increased, it was inevitable that quality would be shaped by mass taste. Television was designed to sell cars and tobacco, not to effect Aristotelian *katharsis*.

Before considering the development of script material for this medium, it will be helpful to look at the structure of program development generally.

The networks, which sell time as magazines sell space, produce most of their own news and public-affairs shows, Accordingly, it has been difficult for independent producers to sell "documentaries"—although there are plenty of exceptions. I will therefore be dealing principally with "entertainment" in what follows.

The key words are "package" and "packager." Though frequently misunderstood, they are fundamental.

Somebody has to furnish a completed show for telecast. Whoever does this—nearly always a corporation—is the packager. The totality of elements constituting the completed show is the package. These will be the usual components of any such enterprise: actors, writers, directors, production personnel, the lot. The packager is their *employer*. As such it will be responsible for making payment subject to withholding tax, for union compliances, for carrying insurance, for doing all the things an employer-company is supposed to do, and for furnishing a completed program to another company which is "buying" this program.

Another way of looking at it is to consider who are *not* packagers. The larger talent agencies are not, even though they represent service and are identified with packages; their producer-clients are the packagers. Individual staff producers are not packagers either; the companies that employ them perform that function.

An odd case is the split package, where one company furnishes certain specific program elements and a different company furnishes the remaining elements. A classic pattern has the "above-the-line" elements, generally the artistic people whose work actually appears on the screen, furnished by A, and the "below-the-line" elements, such as stage crews, furnished by B. Sometimes even the above-the-line people are divided in two groups and employed by different companies for the same show. Originally, tax considerations were behind this sort of thing; a star found himself in such a high income bracket that he insisted on delivering himself and part of the cast, or the writers or director, as employees of his own corporation so as to avail himself of the lower corporate tax rate without running the risk of being treated as a personal holding company. When legitimate, it works.

The next thing is to identify the packager's customers. These generally would be the networks, or local stations, or sponsors acting through advertising agencies, or occasionally a government agency. They are often the final source ordering programs. One pleasing feature they generally have in common is solvency. Whether your show sells to C.B.S. or to General Motors, you will not worry about checks bouncing. In this one respect at least, television is more bracing than the theatre.

Besides packagers and their customers, a third layer exists—the distributors. Only the large packagers have sales forces and distribute their own product. Generally, sponsors have not done much in that line, being content in the past with the right to one network-showing and one summer repeat. Networks have been distributing products for years, but their rights to continue doing so have been challenged. Finally, there are distributing companies as such, who "sell Memphis" when shows are distributed locally, i.e., syndicated.

Except for the odd customer, such as a foundation, these are the top layers of television. Each of them has constituent parts: from one point of view networks are station groupings, distributors are traveling salesmen, packagers are *artistes*.

Television's "Establishment" has an insatiable appetite for all sorts of script material: it needs series and "specials," game, panel and quiz shows, comedy-variety programs and documentaries, anthologies and feature films, not to mention formats, connecting devices and theme songs. It reminds one of certain burrowing mammals who must eat all the time or they perish. In such circumstances they cannot always be fastidious about diet.

How then is literary property developed for the Establishment? There are several ways. Leaving aside news broadcasts, sports and other material which may or may not require permission to broadcast but are not based essentially on copyright, I submit five examples:

The first example is literary material created originally for television, in this case, a proposed series.

The second concerns adaptation from the theatre, for telecast as a special.

In the third we consider adaptation from a novel, for a series.

The fourth example is a spin-off from one series to another, with added ingredients stirred in for flavor.

The fifth lays out a sample writer's arrangement involving services as well as rights in a comedy-variety show.

In the first example somebody wants to create, develop and sell a series to the television Establishment. Since the Establishment is a bit Kafkaesque, as the saying goes, I borrow the name Josef K for my protagonist.

The first thing about K is his lack of creative talent.

His object is to be a producer but he requires something to produce. After the most earnest musing he decides on a format, which might be a family dominated by Mother, or a man tracking down another man, or life in one of the learned professions. None of this sounds quite original, so he combines all three and invents a catchy title. Now he has got something, namely an "idea."

The next step is to get somebody to blow life into this idea and prepare a written presentation for the networks, or advertising agencies, or whatever part of the Establishment is best known to him. A pilot script would be useful too, but it means engaging a writer and this becomes expensive. Therefore K goes to an experienced production assistant whom he knows from a previous series and pays $350, or $500, or whatever he can work out, to get his format written up as a presentation. On counsel's advice he has the production assistant sign a paper releasing to K all rights in the presentation and in all material, including new characters, interpolated by his associate. Now, possibly, the idea has become property.

At this point, K or his agent makes appointments with independent production companies, advertising agencies, and networks. One production company makes an offer to take a free six-month option, which K declines. One agency undertakes to show the presentation to one of its clients who is looking for partial sponsorship of a nighttime series, but a long time goes by with no answer. Finally, one of the networks commissions a step deal.

What the network agrees to is essentially this: K is to receive $10,000 to cover the costs of a half-hour pilot script; rather than commit the full amount, however, the network maintains the right to inspect the script in its various stages of construction—after outline, first draft, and whatever the then current union agreement permits. At any of these points the network may bow out, paying something closer to $2,000 than $10,000 for their mistake. K (or his writer) owns the material written that far along, but sometimes must pay the script money back to the network out of first proceeds derived from sale of this material elsewhere.

If the network likes what it sees, then it will proceed to pilot and perhaps (if sponsorship is found) to series. All of this has to be worked out beforehand in a package agreement. This agreement is all K has to show so far. His writer keeps the $10,000 which the network has paid. K's package agreement with the network covers everything that may happen for years to come.

If my depiction of K seems irreverent it is because too many people dream up original series ideas instead of practicing crafts for which they might be better suited. When professionals do the conjuring we occasionally get something better. ("East Side, West Side" and "The Defenders" were original television concepts that aimed high and impressed reviewers.)

There is a special form of series created originally for television, the File series. By "File," I mean something based on the opening (usually "for the first time") of the files of some interesting organization. It might be one of the medieval London guilds like the Fishmongers or Pewterers, although I doubt whether these stories would command a very large audience aside from members of these honorable crafts. The Sheriff's office in Black Gulch sounds more like a winner. I have been connected with several File-story transactions myself, one based on the O. S. S. of World War II and the other based on a celebrity service that tells subscribers where prominent persons may be found at almost any time.

In a File series, you have to get written clearances from those people in the files who are living. With this sobering reflection I return to that purer art form, the series created originally for television. K, our protagonist, has a package agreement. It brings him along step by step, with fresh funds available each time only if he has passed the preceding hurdle. His package agreement, or his company's, falls into the classic pattern and will be outlined as one of four program arrangements sharing a common structure.

Our second example illustrating how literary property is developed for television concerns adaptation of a play for telecast as a special. The special, once known as a "spectacular," is a single program as distinct from a series. A nice point is whether it should be called a special when it comprises one episode in an anthology series—the Something-or-Other Playhouse—introduced by a Hollywood star wearing eyeglasses for the occasion and pretending to read from a children's classic before the action unfolds. Generally it is not thought of that way. A special is something all by itself even when presented in segments.

When you put on a single play for television you deal with an existing and completed property. This is no mere idea to be nursed into acceptance by hiring good writers or rummaging through files. The material exists, and it was written originally to be performed, although not in this medium. Conceivably you will require nothing at all but the rights to the play itself, and not even that if the play is in the public domain. It is likely, however, that somebody may have to adapt it for television (since Aristophanes neglected the break for commercials) and in some cases you will need a translator. When this happens you may either acquire the rights to an existing translation or hire somebody to do a new one. If somebody does a new one you must check carefully to make sure that he is not pirating other translations, since his agreement to hold you harmless may be worth very little.

Clearing television rights in plays frequently stirs up little foreign crises. Different countries protect copyrights for disparate periods of time. An example of what may happen is my own experience with *Hedda Gabler*. I was connected with a three-way production of Ibsen's play done by C.B.S., B.B.C. and American interests. There was a glittering cast starring Ingrid Bergman, Ralph Richardson, Michael Redgrave and Trevor Howard. A translation by Eva LeGallienne was used and cleared properly with a contract for perpetual world rights. Everything looked in order.

We had found out before production began that Ibsen was still protected in Norway and in several European countries having treaties with Norway. This information surprised everyone—Ibsen was long ago—but we saw no reason to negotiate for Norwegian rights with Ibsen's heirs because distribution in Europe was not scheduled to begin until 1963. The Norwegian copyright, according to our reports, ran out in 1962. The B.B.C., who had charge of European distribution, had only to wait. When that year ended they could pick up the Norwegian and other markets previously debarred, without clearance. Meanwhile *Hedda* could be shown in America, England, and other profitable areas.

Then something unexpected occurred, as euphemism would have it. The Norwegian parliament extended Ibsen's copyrights beyond 1962 by passing a new law. Norway and other countries dropped out of the available market areas. I recall hostile letters from Oslo saying that the production of *Hedda* could not go there. A pragmatic solution was found eventually but the B.B.C. in particular had some awkward moments. I suppose the lesson to be learned is to put on nothing but Shakespeare.

Admittedly *Hedda Gabler* was an unusual case. Still it brings out, rather more graphically than I should have liked at the time, what you are in for with plays on television.

A different way of televising plays is to capture their actual performance before a paying audience. Simultaneous broadcast on opening night, however, raises union problems. In fact this entire prospect is so nerve-wracking that we had best go on to our third example.

A third way in which literary property reaches television may be development of a series from a novel. *Peyton Place* in 1965 will come to mind when future historians log this disturbed era.

The point about novels and stories is that characters and

locale make up a running format that, inevitably, goes far afield from the original work. Sherlock Holmes is a classic example. It is a question of rights in characters divorced from their original stories and set into new frames. While in London on *Hedda*, I was requested by somebody else to clear Sherlock Holmes for use in a cartoon episode. It was uncertain legally whether there was any obligation to secure clearance at all, but I was the captive of a previous book I had written in which I argued that the character still was protected even though many of the stories were public domain in the United States. Thus entrapped, I made arrangements with the Conan Doyle estate.

This whole question of characters leads straight to one of the more interesting concepts in literary property—"spin-off." The spin-off is an ingenious way of developing new material for television.

The phrase "spin-off" refers to the extraction of one or more characters from one program or series for use in another. It means transplant, but it may be used equally to describe the result of the act it describes. Thus the new series resulting from spin-off is itself called a spin-off. The expression is also used as a verb. Before dismissing the subject as sheer pedantry, one might reflect on the enormous money available in this area.

The spin-off may be premeditated or spontaneous. If premeditated, some producer uses an existing program as a "showcase" (another key word here) to introduce his wares for next season. In doing so he deliberately builds the showcase episode around his new character designed to be spun off into a second series. Since the framework is there to begin with, he is spared the cost of a pilot. On the other hand, a spin-off may be spontaneous in that nobody brought in a new character specifically for the purpose of transplant. It can just happen; the public likes the neighbor's dog and next season the neighbor's dog rates his own show.

One thing about spin-off is that you must cover the

point in every television contract. Each show is an acorn, and you will not like missing out on the oak.

An example of spin-off is "Honey West," girl investigator and close combat expert. Honey was introduced on an existing A.B.C. series, "Burke's Law," with a spin-off in mind. What makes it more interesting is that she was derived from a book. She was derived too, although less officially, from a popular English series called "The Avengers" in which a woman gave male opponents some painful karate lessons. When the formula worked, and America seemed ready, they brought on Honey West with her own series. "Burke's Law," her original showcase, never was the same. Its hero changed almost immediately from police captain to espionage agent and then disappeared. Honey West temporarily survived the frame that engendered her. She was the spin-off triumphant.

At this point, a brief aside may serve to bring out the complexity of television in contrast to older media. In the publishing field bookmen put into their contracts that they are to get certain percentages of proceeds from any sale of television rights. But what television rights? On this nuance they remain silent. Consequently, if their best novelists make a television sale, the publishers may be locked out of spin-off participation, or at best may have to accept a court's interpretation. The book publishers and theatre people have not done their homework. Even motion picture attorneys, whose paranoia concerning rights is legendary, sometimes forget the surging possibilities of television.

A fifth and last example of developing script material for television involves services as well as rights. I mention the comedy-variety show as the supreme illustration in this respect—matchless in complexity, frenetic in tempo, astonishing in budget. There may be nothing quite like it.

You are paying for new sketches generally, and have Guild problems. There is no point ticking off this season's collective bargaining agreements but you can be sure that residuals and all that are protected. This kind of program grew up under the live-tape Minimum Basic Agreement, not the film one, and the writer traditionally has held on to more rights in this genre. Nobody is likely to "own" anything forever. Rights are governed by an enormous document dividing everything up according to circumstances. Worse, nobody ever knows who wrote what. I was impressed by this last point over a period working with Sid Caesar's organization where seven of the industry's top comedy writers and a creative star held daily conference. Some of the Caesar characters and sketch fragments that emerged were classics. Nevertheless it was never easy sorting out who had done what in connection with re-use. That kind of data never can be put straight by contract. Collaboration is the thief of order.

Some of the Caesar sketches were licensed separately in England and Australia. These transactions were intricate, less so in license terms than in the unscrambling of underlying rights. Luckily the rights turned out pretty much where they belonged. The same was true with early Shari Lewis puppet material. You can easily see, too, how a recurring sketch character would have spin-off lurking in it. Production numbers contain their own possibilities for night clubs. In short, the comedy-variety format may be the pie from which a thousand nightingales burst forth.

A thousand nightingales mean higher taxes. Most of the stars who have their own shows form companies to package them. These companies divide rights in the sketches with teams of writers who help compose them. Such is the most complex source of material for the Establishment. There are others, of course, but news items and ball games are not really literary property. Perhaps wrestling is something close to it, but the industry has not yet come to grips with its unique subtleties.

This list of programming sources is not complete. Obviously a show can be founded on somebody's diary, and a spin-off be carved out of a phonograph album. Nothing is inconceivable, but I have tried to give plausible illustrations. The fundamental themes recur in varied form. Since this is true of contract patterns too, as suggested in the opening chapter, I shall try to show how the seven basic points relate specifically to television. With *Hedda* the stress may be on one thing, with comedy sketches on another, but the points are constant.

Concerning warranties, I should say that in television the whole structure of them is relatively casual. One reason is that there simply is not time to be very elaborate; another is that original formats are unlikely to have copyright histories that have to be fully recited as is done in motion picture sales. Still another reason, possibly the key one, is that packagers traditionally buy broadcasters' liability insurance that protects them, or is designed to protect them, against claims founded on copyright infringement, violations of the right of privacy and other pitfalls.

This is not to say that warranties of originality and so forth are unimportant. I say rather that they generally consume little negotiating time and less paper. Likely as not there will be "hold harmless" language about originality coupled with assurance that the material is free of unlawful matter and available for television. It is a good thing to smoke out whether conflicting uses are outstanding—a theatrical road tour, for example—but the enormous power of television makes that kind of assurance relatively unimportant. One television showing may destroy the market for a play on tour; the contrary is not true, since a live stage performance in Westport is unlikely to drain off much of the mass television audience. This sort of climate makes warranties about other use of the material itself less important than those in media with smaller audiences.

Possibly the two most important things to remember in connection with television warranties are these: first, stay closely in touch with the insurance company on anything to do with claim language; and second, get cross-indemnities from your buyer covering material interpolated by his staff. Perhaps it would be useful to add that scripts should be looked over by counsel in advance of broadcast.

The next point in our running formula is rights. Here nothing is casual at all. On the contrary, television rights rank with nuclear physics in complexity.

Consider first what must be obvious, questions of time and space. For how long a period should the User acquire rights? At the outset a distinction ought to be made between rights in the material itself and rights in actually recorded programs. Once something has been put on film or tape there is usually no time limit fixing the User's rights in that recording. Fair enough, since it is likely he will need forever to recoup costs. What he may lose after an agreed time is *exclusive* rights, but the recorded performance he bought remains his perpetually.

Rights in the literary material such as format are more likely to be limited. Nobody sells an option to a producer with the expectation that one selling season after another will go by with no royalties. If the producer is unable to lay off his rights on a network or sponsor after a season or two, the rights generally revert to the original owner. This is almost certain to be so when the rights have been optioned for a pittance. Even in the event of reversion, though, the producer-User keeps the right to sell off any pilot he may actually have recorded. The Owner may get something from its distribution, keeping his basic series rights as well, if there is any value left in them.

A more difficult time question arises when there is a pilot that sells into a series. Now the Owner has something— a number of shows guaranteed with multiple royalties or whatever. Is the successful User to be rewarded in this case by perpetual rights in the material itself? Probably so, but there is a trap. What if the first cycle turns out a disaster and the series is cancelled? The packager may have undertaken deficit financing and been wounded. The Owner will have gotten only thirteen royalties, or whatever corresponds to the initial network order, plus residuals if these shows are re-played. That may not be enough to vest perpetual rights in his producer-User. Perhaps rights in the material ought to revert so that the Owner can try elsewhere.

Just how many new program episodes ought to be re-quired as a condition of getting perpetual rights, I am in no position to say. Perhaps twenty-six is a fair number, but the subject is not always negotiable.

Different considerations of time may be the subject of brisk exchange when established plays are televised. A play-wright may be delighted to have his work put on tape and exhibited on a dozen American stations by syndication. As against that there is always the chance of a West End stage production, although nothing has yet been arranged. One thing he may do is grant rights to exhibit once in each listed market within a year. This restriction, however, solves only a minor part of his problem, which is geographical in essence. Therefore we turn from considerations of time to considera-tions of space.

In the main, television buyers require world rights. The foreign market has become too important to be left out, and there are costs to be recouped if not profits to be made. Special properties such as plays would be the main excep-tion. The playwright may stipulate "Never in London," to prevent conflict with something better for himself, but this is an infrequent proviso. Highly distinguished writers may get away with it, not so much because of the esteem in which people hold them as because of the disinterest their works inspire. A first-rate play can be guaranteed to draw smaller audiences than will the moderately well made comedy series. Therefore some prestige sponsor, anxious to improve its image, can afford to draw maps showing where his master-piece may or may not play.

Geography plays an even larger role in the determination

of payments. The Owner may arrange to be paid $X for one run throughout the United States, Canada, Bermuda and Puerto Rico, whatever the original territory comprises according to contract. Thereafter his buyer may play London, or Stockholm, or anywhere else with no restrictions, but he pays more for each area.

At a party launching a new series I was approached by a network official requesting rights to show the series in Tiajuana, Mexico, which they had left out of the contract. Tiajuana was vital because their San Diego station was linked with it. The concession was made at no additional cost, but the anecdote is not reproduced here for *auld lang syne*. Geography is a prime consideration. World rights are one thing, world rights all at the same price may be another.

Another rights question is the number of media encompassed by the grant. Assuming additional payment can be worked out for each separate use, is the Owner willing to part (even for a time) with rights in pay-television, projection in theatres, school showings by closed circuit, a separate phonograph album of the show? With specials in the East, the history has been restrictive. More often than not Users are allowed only to record on tape for free network television. Without the Owner's consent there will be no pay-television, no initial syndication, no release in theatres, possibly no film, nothing but tape sold in the traditional way. Other uses in schools, ships, planes, even exhibition for the Armed Forces, may be withheld although networks may require some of these things in the package agreement.

West Coast demands generally are more extensive. The major studios demand every possible right, even stage rights, or at the very least, elaborate restrictions against the Owner's use of what little he is permitted to hold back. One buyer may be equipped to make a feature picture or a television series out of the same property, even to finance and co-produce a Broadway musical derived from the script. Frequently all the Owner can do is share profits in the media granted. ("Wrested" may be a better word than "granted" since nobody wants all of his eggs in one basket.)

When rights are reserved there is usually a time limit preconditioning their exercise. It might be the first network telecast, this in turn being subject to a time limit determining reversion to the Owner. With specials the User may occasionally be met with demands by the author for an escape clause if he is offered a motion picture sale. Even if the author is willing to return option payments, this sort of thing is impossible once his buyer has made production commitments.

A final point is spin-off ownership. I have already dealt with this subject at some length, noting that extricable component segments of one special or series may come to life in a new series divorced from the original. All sorts of questions arise, ranging from definitions to profit shares. The financial arrangements are a separate point but at this stage I should like to say one or two things about definitions.

Under present practice there is more to it than whether or not the first Owner gets compensation out of a spin-off. That contest may be resolved by dividing spin-off series into two sub-categories. In one category the spin-off is based on and utilizes something substantial—usually one or more characters—from the original property. When this happens the Owner has a continuing share in the new series. In the other category the spin-off is planted fortuitously in the Owner's series as a convenient showcase and the new series has nothing substantial from the original except what was planted this one time. When this happens the Owner gets nothing from the new series.

I am tempted to mention still other instances where the number of characters extracted becomes a point for negotiation, and spin-off derived from a previous spin-off is closely considered. Worth mentioning, too, is that fictional characters are not inevitably the bridge from one series to another. An imaginary locale or device might be spun off and reborn for a season or two elsewhere. Similarly a character trait might be grafted on to another fictional character under a new name. I have seen that done more than once, although nobody called it a spin-off. All one can say is pay attention to all of the chess pieces. The pawn may become a queen.

The question of services requires familiarity with whatever Guild rules may be currently applicable.

I have before me an enormous document reflecting present trade practice in connection with rights to a series pilot. The main paper is a ten-page form, with various blanks filled in, employing a writer to do a pilot script based on a format of his own creation. The format is annexed as Exhibit I. The form requires that the writer will furnish a treatment by a fixed date for $5,000. Thereafter the company may exercise an option to have him write the final teleplay for another $5,000. If, despite exercise of the option, the packager-User has not made firm arrangements by such and such a time to produce a pilot, or even if he has made these arrangements but has not commenced principal photography of the pilot within a later time limit, and accepted a firm order for production of at least twelve new series episodes by another time limit, not to mention going into actual production within still another time limit, the property reverts.

If it does not revert, and if the series is "based substantially on the final text of the story and teleplay furnished by Writer hereunder," the writer is to be Script Consultant and/or Associate Producer (packager's choice) for $5,000 more on the pilot and $1,500 per new program throughout the whole span of the initial network program order, probably thirteen shows with an option for somewhere between thirteen and twenty-six more in the first year. A form governing his services as Script Consultant (which becomes Supervisor) or Associate Producer is annexed to the contract as Exhibit II.

The packager then has a series of yearly options for the

same services subject to 10 percent annual salary increases.

Throughout any first two years of production the writer is guaranteed that he will write, or at least be paid for, three out of each thirteen new program episodes, at $3,500 each or the "top of the show" rate (i.e., the highest price paid any writer on the series—a most favored nations concept borrowed from diplomacy), waiving his supervisory or production salary with each show he writes.

The rest of it is all about profit shares, which are diminishable if the series is not "based substantially on the final text of the story and teleplay furnished by Writer hereunder" (a formula that usually creates controversy). I will be dealing with profit shares later on, but I have summed up the arrangement for services as a sample of current custom. Owners are tying themselves in with property sales. They turn up as writers of three out of thirteen new episodes, as associate producers, script supervisors and so forth. Services are tied in with rights to a literary composition. Some of the services are governed by union collective bargaining agreements, others are not.

The degree to which services are exclusive is another standard issue. Protection for the User against his writer's endorsing or rendering services for competitive sponsors similarly has to be spelled out. When services are tied in you will have to conform exclusivity requirements to the package agreement at the very least.

Even more complex is payment. Let me return for a moment to the papers before me. Our Owner-creator-consultant-supervisor-associate producer has a share of net profits derived from all uses of the series including merchandising and theatrical release. If the series is based on his teleplay— there is no use quoting the whole formula once again—he has 25 percent of the packager's share (which is to be deemed not under 50 percent of all profits) reducible to 20 percent if and to the extent profit shares are committed to others such as stars and the director. If the series is based only on his raw property, but not on his teleplay, he can be put down to 15 percent. Needless to add, there are residuals based on his royalties besides, in this case 140 percent of his applicable per-program royalty spread over five runs throughout the world. Spin-off royalties and profit shares correspondingly reflect the degree in which his teleplay did or did not "sell the series."

On the definition of profits I have a ten-page document before me reflecting a set of current objections to a typical studio definition of that term:

(a) There is no spelling out of overhead deductions, for example whether stage space, department head salaries, equipment and *force majeure* contingencies are included.

(b) A production fee and supervisory executive fee are charged in addition to overhead.

(c) There are no separate accounting units (with no production loss recoupment) with respect to foreign language versions, subsidiary rights, merchandising and spin-off series.

(d) It is not clear enough that profit shares apply with respect to all uses of the property, not just recorded programs.

(e) There is no "most favored nations" clause.

(f) The "Statute of Limitations" on accountings should be at least eighteen months after the first annual report.

(g) Infringement recoveries from third persons should be included in gross receipts.

(h) The lower (10 percent) distribution fee should apply to any fifty-station exhibition as a national sale, and not only on first run.

(i) Canadian network sales distribution fees should be 25 percent and Canada should be within the 10 percent fee if part of the United States network sale or bought by a United States sponsor.

(j) The foreign distribution fee should be 40 percent, not 50 percent.

(k) Distribution fees for theatrical exhibition should be 35 percent for the United States, United Kingdom, and Malta; 40 percent elsewhere.

(l) The cost of laboratory work should be at a competitive rate with discounts passed on to the participant.

(m) There should be a limit on advertising, e.g., 3 percent of gross excluding domestic network gross.

(n) Counsel fees for infringement actions should be "reasonable."

(o) Outright sales should be accountable.

There is a great deal more, some of it dealing with charges in unfreezing blocked funds, and other sections on accounting procedures, all of it reflecting suspicion.

Generally not very much can be done with net profits definitions. Studios deduct their overhead charges, distribution fees and the lot, but I might usefully repeat several things Owners might try with some reasonable chance of success. One is to make sure on *whose* share of profits his own share is hinged, not to be less than X percent of the total. Another is a "most favored nations" clause to ensure the same definition of net profits that the buyer gets from his distributor. This is useful especially in sales to independent producers unable to distribute their own product. And finally there are normal rights to inspect books and records relating to the particular venture.

I mentioned earlier that pay-television is more likely to afford Owners a share of gross rather than net profits. In the history of television thus far, that mode of payment has been unusual. Generally, the formula is royalties plus residuals. If services are involved, there are salaries and residuals on writing "salary," and with creators or other rights owners, a share of net profits besides. Most of it is contingent, some of it optional. All of it is rather hard to define in a way that will please everyone.

A last payment pattern worth remembering is connected with foreign licensing of scripts and formats as distinct from the recorded program itself. There the traffic is light, but you can generally work out sensible pay formulas based on the running time in minutes of each sketch if less than a complete dramatic script or format is being licensed. If the Australians or other browsers want time to pick and choose from a number of sketches, you may be able to arrange a "reading fee" for their option, within a fixed time period, to select the desired materials at an agreed price per head with residuals for subsequent runs. There may be no reason that the reading fee should be deemed an advance against purchase price. The material is being tied up and they are paying for time. This point is disputable but I have seen it resolved favorably for the Owner often enough to distinguish this case from advances for books and plays. Foreign licensing is less predetermined by custom.

Another point is control. There is little to say about creative control because television, generally, does not reserve any to the author. There are too many levels of the Establishment, each with its own veto rights. Creative approval clauses may smash the show. I have seen several with local programs, but even there they are out of accord with industry structure.

More in point is control of the rights as such. Collaborators have to set this out unequivocally in their agreements before being sent back by prospective buyers to clear everything up. After that, packagers control rights, yielding them in turn to distributors who finance them. Only direct sponsor sales are likely to leave syndication in the packager's hands. Networks have been taking that on themselves, subject to sharing profits. Subsidiary rights in other media may be held back more successfully.

Billing credit is not solely a question of ego. Actual rights in the material as well as payments may be shaped by what sort of credit appears on the screen. In an earlier example I mentioned how royalties and profits might be greater or lesser, under a contract, depending on whether or not someone's pilot script was the basis of a series sale. In such a case, determination concerning credit for "teleplay" might loom large no matter who had been promised "Created by" credit. Then too, there is the usual fussing about size and placement. Credit on a "single frame" is the prize in this medium.

Another matter requiring delicacy comes up in connection with comedy-variety programming. When a sketch is re-used but changed, the safest thing to say is "Based on" material or a sketch by so and so. In that way he gets credit but has a less valid complaint about script changes. He can say that all the good bits are his as the original writer. Everything that went wrong resulted from being "based on" instead of a line for line reproduction of perfection.

Finally, there is the question of assignment. Television does not make very much of this point, but the User had better have his right to assign. In a strictly technical sense, licensing material for broadcast is something less than true assignment. What increases the pressure is that networks and other Users may have "takeover" provisions in their package agreements which require assignment of all rights if they take over production. Obviously too, the original packager may want to do some juggling for his own reasons or to accommodate a star who insists on co-producing through a joint venture.

Usually it is not difficult to get the right to assign. Whatever the law is, many rights owners insist on a provision that the User remain liable if his assignee defaults. Fair enough, however they work out the definition of "defaults." Nobody can shirk his responsibility completely.

Volume and quick tempo are the hallmarks of literary property dealings in television. In no other medium do obscure script rights turn to gold so dramatically, or as part of such complex arrangements. A spin-off spun off from a spin-off is actually a point worth considering in business negotiation even though it has the sound of medieval scholasticism more fitting in the lecture hall. Dealing in television rights can make any man into a philosopher. Not many of these conversions will be permanent, but the astounding thing is that they should occur at all.

THE THEATRE

DRAMA BEGAN AS A RITUAL DESIGNED TO INFLUENCE, BY imitation, the cycle of the seasons and the rebirth of nature. There are many in the commercial theatre for whom return to this ancient purpose would be highly fitting.

The theatre is scarcely an industry at all. Only a few producers and managers constitute a continuing Establishment in this field. Some among this management are amateurs with a sense of artistic mission. All too often they turn up on the top rank, especially off-Broadway, only to vanish after the play closes, leaving not a rack behind, except for the dishonored check, their trademark.

There are successes in the theatre that ring clear through the world, but they are frequently isolated ventures, not the product of a continuing business enterprise administered by professionals with a revolving treasury. Specific partnership structures end at the same time a play does, although successful producers command much of the same investment following with each new play. As in so many endeavors, professionalism is everything.

The few instances of success are so notable, and the opportunities they afford to the creative so rewarding that the commercial theatre cannot be left out of a book about literary property.

In present practice the author has a good deal to say about how his play is put on. That one element is unique

53

in the performing arts. In past eras (for the theatre has plenty of history to balance its want of mercantile soundness) quite the opposite was true. The business end of it was more like Hollywood.

Records of how things were done in Shakespeare's time are preserved in Henslowe's *Diary* and the *Alleyn Papers*. One surmises that production costs (considered relatively) were lower, even though a 1598 inventory of the Lord Admiral's Men listed items such as "1 Rock," "1 Mouth of Hell" and "a Boar's Head." The author sold all rights to the producing company and his play could be altered without advance written approval. At the turn of the century, *circa* 1600, play fees were rising from £6 to £11.

Later, we begin seeing some familiar patterns in the subsidiary rights area. An agreement dated October 29, 1696, between Colley Cibber and Christopher Rich for the production of *Woman's Witt*, includes this provision:

> And the said Mr. Cibber is to have the sole Benefitt of Printing such play: But he is not to suffer it to bee Printed till a month next after it shall be first acted.

Leaping ruefully to the present century—that is, from the manager's viewpoint—we find the commercial theatre in considerable distress. Government and foundation grants are needed to pump funds into this hallowed art form. Important theatre groups are springing up in all sorts of unlikely towns while Broadway languishes and even the West End looks pale. Nevertheless, it is too soon to suggest that the established centers are doomed. They are still Mecca.

Production groupings in the theatre generally are improvised and fluid. That would be the first thing an anthropologist would note down in any survey of its bizarre rituals. The Rock of Gibraltar and Bank of England are no models for its Establishment. More likely than not the anthropologist would find plays presented by A (whose name he has heard) in association with B (known only to B's parents) by arrangement with C (who was bought out). The key figure in a sense is B. This person brings in some of the money.

Unfortunately, money-raising is a key function in the theatre. Though this is true of other arts of communication, the feeling is different. Either a network will finance your *Hamlet* for television or it will not (more likely the latter). Once it does, all of the money is from one source, and the check will clear. In the theatre one raises money on a continuing basis. There are the embarrassing little parties, the backers' auditions and telephone calls to close friends. Financing is done through a multiplicity of sources and becomes a way of life.

In all fairness, some of this has been changing. In television, it is harder and harder to negotiate sufficient financing to meet budget requirements. Theatre money, on the other hand, may be available from a record company which acquires cast album rights or a film company doing a "pre-production deal" to obtain film rights. Still, the theatre is largely "passing the hat." Accordingly B, mentioned earlier, gets credit as co-producer.

Usually, a limited partnership is created to produce a play. The general partner is the producing team who receive half of the profits and are individually (unless incorporated) liable for losses. A number of limited partners put up the funds and subdivide, in proportion to their investments, the remaining half of profits. They are not liable for losses beyond what they put in, although some partnership agreements may make them subject to "overcall" in a predetermined amount. Limited partners have to be careful, however. When they authorize expenditure of their investment as "front money," before the whole capitalization is in, frequently they demand more than their proportionate share of the investors' end. This is all very well until they acquire billing credit and production authority. When this happens they may be held liable for losses with the producers.

Life is not all that bleak for the general partners. Besides profits they take one or more percentages of gross together with "office charges" in a fixed weekly amount. Generally, disclosure of their arrangements is required by SEC regulations, since public offerings are involved, and by the Attorney-General, since to conceal is human.

Users in the theatre constantly re-group. With each new play there is a new limited partnership for its production. Top flight producers may themselves form a continuum between one play and the next; loyal backers may follow the same management in successive productions; proceeds from touring companies may come in for years. Structurally, though, production units in the theatre differ from those in other media. There is no such thing here as the same publishing house producing all of the books by grateful X. There may be something quite like it with accredited producers, but the technical difference is important because it shapes the market for literary property.

The right to assign becomes vital in this kind of structure. Anyone taking a play option had better be sure to have rights to assign—as many as he can get. For one thing, he eventually will assign all of his rights to the producing partnership. For another, he will want co-producers with money, and beyond all that, he will need the right to let some of the creative people inherit his position if he abandons production. Assignment rights will be mentioned again later, but their relevance in a structure of clustered partnerships is clear. The theatre is founded on quickly improvised alliance.

Where does the quickly improvised alliance get its plays from? Original works composed for live performance before a paying audience are only one of the sources. Sometimes you will have adaptations from another medium. The basic work might be a book, as in the case of several stage adaptations of *Pickwick Papers*. It might be a television show such as "The Miracle Worker" or "Middle of the Night." It might be a comic strip character such as "Li'l Abner" or "Superman." It might even be a motion picture.

Optioning a work which has previously been a motion picture makes an unappetizing bundle unless film rights can be cleared. However modest the producer's ambitions, he will find it difficult attracting adaptors and investors without the possibility of a film sale; and the company owning film rights will be in a position to do some stiff bargaining. In addition to film rights in the new play version, they may require album and publication rights for their record subsidiary and a share of gross and net proceeds from the play. Cash payments in advance, mercifully, are not always made a condition. Realism, not gallantry, is the rationale.

Several examples illustrate how literary material is developed for Users—in this case, play producers.

In the first example, so-called "first class rights" in a straight play are optioned.

In the second, there is a license of British rights in the same work.

The third example is a Broadway musical based on existing characters.

The fourth is a Broadway musical based on a teleplay.

In the fifth, we consider an off-Broadway revue derived from a magazine format.

Defining "first class rights" has been the subject of lively disagreement. London contracts (at least those made in America) frequently require spelling out the names of particular theatres in the definitions. In past years I have seen productions at the Royal Court and the Lyric Theatre in Hammersmith that were first class by any standard. Still it was often necessary to mention one or both as exceptions in contracts that required production in the West End.

The American problem has been even more perplexing. The proliferation of theatre groups in Minnesota, Texas and other exotic places has made it difficult to know what should be considered first class besides Broadway.

Whether or not a production is first class, is important in shaping the author's contract. Traditionally, the Dramatists

Guild Minimum Basic Production Contract has governed first class productions. Challenged as to jurisdiction every now and then, it still serves as the mold for business custom. Theoretically, a playwright was best protected under a contract for first class production of his play. This was scarcely his chief concern but his representatives would be quite aware of the point.

A clear account of the position requires mention of the word "theoretically" once again. Saying that first class production theoretically protects authors because of the Guild simply means that a playwright *off* Broadway is likely to get just as attractive terms, only with smaller rewards. His representatives see to that by incorporating Guild provisions—by force coupled with analogy.

First class rights in a straight play are by no means the simplest illustration of how literary material is developed for the theatre. They come first, but we bog down on definition. The rest is fairly straightforward.

The author submits his play to a producer, or a producer approaches the author, and an option is granted. Definitions aside, the rest appears simple.

At least one variation, however, merits additional digression. It happens occasionally that a performer commissions material specially tailored for his own interpretation on the stage. Whether or not others appear in it, and notwithstanding that it may be more a succession of sketches than a true play, he has special problems and opportunities here.

The performer is more than likely an actress. Her bill may be called, "An Evening with Emma Frankenstein," or something equally as glamorous—that would be the sort of bill I have in mind.

Ladies in this situation may have special problems. For one thing they are unlikely to have many starring roles in the future; thus every word of the commissioned text becomes an heirloom for future display. For another, bits and pieces of other tailored material find their way into the new production only to vest, merged with the newer segments, in the writer. An actress who allows this to happen may lose control of her best showcase forever. Each booking thereafter, from Berlin to Bombay, may require the writer's permission secured by substantial payments.

As against that, there may be special opportunities to avoid all that and the Guild formulas as well. If our actress commissions an "Act" tailored to no medium in particular, she may come out the owner. Copyright law recognizes ownership in the employer of works written by employees in the scope of their employment. Actually that legalistic an approach is impractical here, but it provides framework. Writers expect royalties nowadays, and only the worst hack would let any rights for live performance go outright. Therefore the "Act" notion becomes interesting.

What the actress may do is engage writers to furnish her with an act suitable for night clubs and all media. If she performs it in cabarets they get X; if she performs it on television they get Y; on the stage, Z, and so on. The formula is rather like that of a concert tour—a succession of bookings one place after the other and not really a Broadway engagement at all. If fortuitously it opens on Broadway there are still plenty of other things that might have happened and may still. The actress controls the material and her writers are paid however it is used. There is nothing uncivilized about this structure.

In our second example, an American play is licensed to United Kingdom management for West End production. Fortunately for New Yorkers the traffic is just as heavy going in the other direction. Whether Sloane Square is part of the West End has been gone into pretty thoroughly, and other problems to consider when plays cross the Atlantic will be dealt with later, but there is one that ought to be brought out now. This is the question of the author who writes himself in for a paid flight with expenses during his London sojourn. The director and choreographer (with musicals) have the option to go along as well. Once there they will officially exercise creative controls on a scale reserved only to artists working in the theatre. The original stars may or may not make the crossing, but those who created the property are unlikely to stay away.

A third example is the Broadway musical based on existing characters. Some of the characters may come from comic strips, others from classics. The "pure" characters grant (with no accompanying story rights) is rare, but I have done at least two of them and suspect the practice may become less uncommon.

One or two pitfalls await people who deal in fictional characters. To begin with, nobody seems able to define characters, and while I am personally sure that a well delineated character is the same property whether or not you change his name, not everyone agrees. Falstaff is Falstaff in several plays, to cite an instance of Elizabethan spin-off, and we are going to recognize him even if he appears next time under the name Copperfield.

That there might be pitfalls of quite a different sort occurred to me—one of those fleeting morbid fancies—as I was watching a C. P. Snow novel performed on the stage. If you have read more than one of Snow's Cambridge novels you will remember that individual characters, or at least some of them, such as Jago and old Gay, could be left out and the writing would still be memorable. This is true because the Cambridge community itself is made a protagonist. Yet Cambridge itself, unlike Brigadoon, is no fictitious locale, and this suggested the problem. What if one were putting on a play of the kind I have been talking about, based on a Snow novel, and found somebody else in the theatre next door doing another play about the same characters? Not very likely, since he might have optioned or at least restricted the next stage use of the same characters. But what if the characters were different— no Jago, no Gay—and the protagonist locale the same? Box office prospects would be bleak. Security might require tying up all of the Cambridge novels, present or future, but this is a bit much when a novel about Cambridge might be peopled with just greengrocers. Perhaps the answer would be tying up rights in all of the author's novels about Cambridge and dons together but not separately.

This line of reflection may prove fruitful in some future negotiation. More certainly, it spoils theatre-going for the negotiator.

And now to a fourth example—a teleplay turned into a musical. One experience with this genre (which never opened) has persuaded me of its suitability in this chapter, solely on the ground of complexity. There is enough of every problem extant to please everyone. Who owns the series format? Who owns the characters? Where are the motion picture rights? Who gets what in theatrical production? Who gives the warranties? Are any television rights left for the Broadway producer? What happens with new characters introduced by the librettist? Let us move quickly to the fifth and last example.

An off-Broadway revue based on a magazine format is far enough off the beaten track to invite attention. I include it to bring out the diversity of possible source material for the theatre. There is more to it than just plays. Literary property may be found in all sorts of odd places.

When I was asked to work out the stage rights to *Mad Magazine* I had glimpses of uncharted seas, not to mention premonitions of shipwreck. Only the first was justified. "The Mad Show" was a hit. Its success was well justified by the high level and scathing tenor of its songs and sketches, that much is clear. Whether others in the audience shared my musings on many of the fine points of literary property suggested by this show is less easily established.

Let us consider next how these samples of modern stage sources relate to our seven basic contract points.

The question of warranties becomes a whodunit. The central issue when you have collaborators is dividing responsibility according to what segment was contributed by which writer. Usually the writer of the book furnishes warranties only with respect to the book, a co-lyricist only with respect to his own words, and so on until you get down to the underlying rights owner in cases of adaptation. Here the problems with chain of title are more intricate.

Returning to the musical based on a teleplay, there is a line of reflection that should ordinarily suggest itself before anyone holds harmless anyone else under a warranty clause.

The basic property is one program episode in a series. Therefore the writer or writers of that episode surely have some sort of position which has to be checked. If new consents are required on their part, obtain new warranties for the stage version, but only to the extent that their teleplay is used.

Somebody else, possibly, owns the series format as distinct from the one program episode. All of the basic characters probably came with the format and were merely used in a new story by the writers of each episode. Therefore the format owner has some sort of position which has to be checked, with attendant responsibilities concerning warranties.

If the format turns out to have been founded on still another property such as a novel or screenplay, the clearance process continues further. As additional grants become necessary, so do symmetrical warranties covering the element granted.

An always perplexing question is whether it is wise or not to require inspection of underlying rights documents. If you are buying from somebody solvent, and he is willing to warrant certain things to be true, you may weaken your position by snooping through old papers and finding the contrary. Then you may be on notice of defects in the chain of title and be debarred from complaining about them. On the other hand, you may find such defects that you will decide to withdraw from negotiations completely, warranty or no warranty. Generally, I should think the latter procedure more professional. Similarly, on the seller's end, one ought to be sure that a covering letter in the file confirms what the buyer has seen. Surprise has no legitimate place in these transactions.

A last thought on the subject of warranties in play contracts is suggested by the word "title" itself. Here I mean the name of the play, and people who ought to know better sometimes demand warranties that the name is clear for use exclusively with that play. Nobody can give such warranties. Titles are not protected by copyright. They may acquire legal protection through secondary meaning, that is, through identification with a play or author, but that justifies only a lesser warranty: that so far as you know, the name is clear; that nobody has yet challenged it; that you have not licensed its use to five other producers—that kind of hedged assurance. Nobody can guarantee ownership of a name in these circumstances.

Our second point is rights. Off-Broadway a producer will want the option to present the play *on* Broadway, or otherwise as a first class production. It may not always be in the playwright's interest to accommodate him, but the point should be covered one way or the other. Obviously the producer who gets more has to pay more for it when the time comes.

Rights in a play generally follow a fixed pattern. There is less flexibility than in television. In fact, there is relatively little bargaining on this crucial point because everyone knows in advance how it will come out. On Broadway (as distinct from a limited engagement at a local repertory theatre), the producer must be reasonably sure of certain things. Without them he may find it difficult capitalizing his play.

Generally the rights granted follow a structure of producer's options which may in turn be lost by the producer if he fails to accomplish certain things within fixed time periods.

The producer will have this sort of Guild-shaped exclusive option: to produce the play on the "speaking stage" (a case of animism, but that is the phrase used) in the United States and Canada and acquire the author's services in connection therewith. Depending on what he pays, the producer is likely to have a year to open the play or lose it, subject to extension for up to six months for standard difficulties such as getting a suitable theatre.

It becomes apparent that there is a sharp difference between theatre practice and custom in the camera industries. If the producer has produced the play for twenty-one consecutive performances in New York, or sixty-four out-of-town performances within eighty days (or a mixed bag on this order) or deposited $6,000 for the author's benefit (subject to return if the play is abandoned) then the producer acquires certain additional rights. These additional rights range from the exclusive right to present the play in the "British Isles" to participation in the monies derived from subsidiary rights retained by the author: motion picture rights and (in the United States and Canada) radio, television, second class touring performances, foreign language performances, condensed and tabloid versions, concert tour versions, commercial uses (the toy and game syndrome), grand opera and (with qualifications) stock and amateur. In those circumstances the producer will also have certain approval rights with respect to rights licensed by the author.

Even then nothing has vested permanently except the right to share proceeds. The producer must keep up the good work. If he falters he must rely on "reopening rights" within four and a half months after the close of the initial first class run, making additional payments for more time. The point is that he is dealing with live things, not film. He owns nothing permanently merely by virtue of exercising an option. On the contrary he must keep doing something or be sent out of the game.

Normal sources of revenue include the cast album (with musicals), road performances, and the less easily defined bus and truck tours. Even souvenir programs can occasion the payment of huge advances.

The key word is "services," and it is one of the rights a producer gets when he options a play. The author comes along with the play in the Dramatists Guild type of production we have been considering. Automatically then, you have an artificial situation. There are mandatory ground rules instead of variable custom. In a discussion of literary property it remains inappropriate to dissect fully the standard industry-wide agreement of the moment, but awareness of its applicability should be noted.

A better example of unfettered rights-dealing is the license for British production. I have a recent contract in front of me and its terms were negotiated solely by the parties involved, that is to say, without reference to anyone else's standards. It is a purer literary property arrangement than anything you are likely to see on Broadway except for the previously mentioned "Act." At the same time one can only use the comparative, "purer," because elements of former service contracts keep coming into it. The author has certain rights, the original director has the option to do the play over again in London, and so forth. Still the license itself better exemplifies trafficking in rights without supervision by a third party.

In this British license agreement, the people in London are given the exclusive right to present the play as a first class production in the United Kingdom and the Republic of Eire. They have six months to open it in the West End and they must run it for twenty-one consecutive performances (Guild memories weave in and out) to avoid reversion of rights. They are supposed to adhere substantially to the text of the play as presented in New York, "except for local regionalisms" (not to mention tautological redundancies) and subject to the author's rights of control.

If they meet all the initial time requirements their license includes first class road companies (Britain and Ireland only) plus a participation in stock and amateur rights there, with other little bonuses like the right to do forty minutes of the play on television or radio for advertising. This broad permission to use television is balanced by a ten-year limit terminating the entire license, no matter what anyone does.

All other rights are reserved in terms verging on paranoia.

The third point, services, was anticipated in our preceding discussion concerning the scope of rights. Theatre tradition itself has made services inevitable, since when you put on a play (unlike a film) the original author usually comes along with it. Playwrights work very hard, sometimes even after the play opens, but pride rather than contract is the reason. In the theatre there is little detailed definition of the author's duties. Not infrequently the producer would like him barred from the theatre.

Minimum Guild terms require payment of an advance against a percentage of gross weekly box office receipts with appropriate statements furnished. Typical minimum has been $2,000 for a year's hold, against a fixed or escalating percentage of gross less deductions for local taxes and occasionally other charges far less ominous than deductions in other media that pay percentages of "net." With straight plays percentages may range between five and ten percent. In a musical the book, music and lyrics might get 2 percent each. Certainly advances and percentages of gross may go considerably higher when the creative people have bargaining position.

When the show gets into trouble there will be tense little meetings in which everyone except actors may agree on a pay cut. Sometimes the waived royalty is merely deferred by agreement, deferred until things look brighter and then recouped according to any number of agreed formulas. Even before trouble sets in, the contracts may call for a royalty increase when production costs are recouped. There is a great feeling of all being in it together.

On the brighter side, what if film rights are sold? Generally the proceeds from subsidiary rights will go 60 percent to the authors collectively and 40 percent to the producer if he fulfilled the conditions for sharing. The producer will get less if the play is a long time being sold to a picture company, but these details are Guild points again and are based on the notion of writing services, not property.

New patterns of payment are evolving, such as the pay formulas for rights owners who are *not* engaged for the rendition of Guild services. Typically, the owner is the novelist whose book is made into a play. His case is even purer property dealing, at least conceptually, than the case of the British play license mentioned earlier. Our novelist does not even have to leave his villa.

His rewards are generally an advance—say $5,000—against 1 percent of gross, or 1½ percent, perhaps subject to increase after recoupment. Where it goes mathematical is on the sale of subsidiary rights. What his contract should say is that he shares in the *author's* share of proceeds in the same proportion that his box office percentage of gross in the theatre bears to all the writing elements, but in no event will the latter be deemed to be more than X percent of gross. Assume that on Broadway the novelist whose work is turned into a musical gets 1 percent of gross weekly box office receipts. The author of the Broadway book gets 2 percent, the composer 2 percent and the lyricist (the world's leading poet represented by the world's meanest agent) 10 percent, a figure grotesquely at variance with the usual 2 percent. We note immediately that it does not cut into the novelist's share during the Broadway run if the lyricist gets 10 percent, since this extraordinary share of gross comes out of somebody else.

Now there is a film sale for $100,000. Of this the

producer gets 40 percent, i.e. $40,000, leaving $60,000 as the composite authors' share to be subdivided. On Broadway, the novelist's royalty bore to the remaining authors' royalties the relation that 1 percent bears to 14 percent. To foreclose this bleak prospect, the novelist's representative would have stipulated that on film sale it would be deemed that no more than 10 percent of gross—even that is rather high—had been paid as royalties to the entire creative group. Contracts with writers of the book, music and lyrics (made afterwards) would be subject to this provision. Therefore the novelist would be assured at least one-tenth of the $60,000 authors' portion of the $100,000 film sale. As underlying rights owner he would get $6,000. A provision against having this share overly diluted proves helpful.

That an underlying rights owner shares pro rata in the composite authors' portion of subsidiary rights proceeds, subject to limits on diluting his own share, is fair and sensible. It is also hard to word and sometimes harder to compute.

An ideal finale bringing in all themes is the example, previously referred to with suitable foreboding, of the musical based on a teleplay. Here are the figures from that contract:

From gross weekly box office receipts from the presentation of the play:

Book	2%
Music	2%
Lyrics	2%
2 contributors of special material	1½%
2 underlying teleplay owners (on recoupment)	½%–1%

From subsidiary rights and advances on British licensing, but subject to exceptions listed afterwards, the following aggregate authors' share after deducting the producer's share:

Book	25%
Music	25%

Lyrics	25%
2 contributors of special material	18¾%
2 underlying teleplay owners	6¼%

The producer waives any share of proceeds from printed publication rights of the libretto with or without lyrics and such proceeds are divided as follows when lyrics are included:

Book	33⅓%
Lyrics	33⅓%
2 contributors of special material	25%
2 underlying teleplay owners	8⅓%

But when lyrics are not included:

Book	50%
2 contributors of special material	37½%
2 underlying teleplay owners	12½%

The cast album itself is a show in microcosm. The authors' 60 percent of cast-album net proceeds after paying the cast, orchestra, and other costs is divided this way:

Book	10%
Music	20%
Lyrics	20%
2 contributors of special material	7½%
2 underlying teleplay owners	2½%

(Proceeds from "small" performing, mechanical and synchronization rights in the separate music and lyrics as distinguished from these elements as part of the play are retained solely by the lyricist and composer.)

In these examples where I mention two of any category, the percentage cited constitutes total payment for the brace.

On the question of control, once again we find the author flourishing as in no other medium. Earlier we saw that in the theatre he keeps more rights and gets to do more arithmetic. Now we shall see that he controls the creative aspects of his play as well.

Dramatists Guild tradition reserves to the playwright a number of vital creative controls. The cast, director, conductor and dance director must be agreeable to him as well as to the producer. After the opening, any replacements of these elements remain subject to mutual consent. As to the play itself, the producer is allowed only to make changes authorized by the author, even with road companies. Any such changes belong to the author.

Control over the rights is very much in the same key. It was previously made clear how many of them the author kept back, subject to sharing proceeds in certain circumstances. Even the British rights are disposed of only with the author's written consent, and subject to creative controls. More often than not the author's agent commissions the producer's share in a sale of film rights. Yet, life is not all that pleasant for playwrights.

In the more industrialized media, work is steadier and initial payments are higher. An author writing in the theatre must be dedicated indeed. The whole picture in this chapter is one of *auctor triumphans*, but the picture reflects contracts more than it does life.

One safeguard for authors adapting a novel or other property is to be sure they inherit what remains of the producer's rights in that property if the producer abandons it. Otherwise writers may spend a year or two working on something they may never be able to present on the stage once the underlying rights vanish. When this happens before the basic work merges with new stage material, under a proper "merger" clause, the adaptors have bleak prospects. They must protect themselves in advance by having the basic rights owner and the producer both agree on their right to inherit the underlying rights. Otherwise nothing is left except brandy and pistol.

With multiple authors a collaboration agreement may fix some voting procedure for the making of decisions on control. In the creative end of it each author may be the one who decides whether his own contribution may be altered.

Off Broadway you may find even more stringent author controls than with first class productions. There are contracts stipulating that the play may be put on only in theatres with a certain minimum number of seats, or where no liquor is served. As against that, the playwright may be earning less than his bootblack. The theatre is more an art than an industry.

That it is not always the most noble art appears in even the briefest consideration of point six, billing credit. The theatre is where most of the in-fighting about size of lettering, color and prominence given somebody's name was most lively. Perhaps this is because the theatre is the oldest of the art forms we are considering. Whether this is the reason or not, jealousy in this field takes picturesque forms.

The usual problems are not only whether one's name belongs over the play's title or under, this with reference to the marquee, but in what sort of advertising the formula must be followed. ABC (alphabetized newspaper) and teaser ads frequently are exempt, but the producer will have to list the author appropriately in media he controls, such as programs, houseboards and wherever else the producer's name appears. Of course billing credit for authors is always a sore point. The stars are what bring people in, usually, even though reviews dealing with the play itself make more of an impression than is true elsewhere.

Finally we return to assignment, important especially in a field where new partnerships are formed with each production.

A producer may assign his rights to a corporate Guild signatory in which he has the controlling interest or of which he is the directing head or to a partnership all of whose general partners are Guild signatories. The producer remains liable and is supposed to file the assignment with the Guild. Technically, that is what you may do with first class productions, although language about co-producing with associates of one's choice usually is put in for good measure.

What goes on among various producers dividing up interests may not be directly connected with literary property. Nevertheless, it is so much part of the background to assignments that a few words on the subject should not be too far off the mark.

At the beginning of this chapter I suggested a typical co-production grouping in which at least one of the partners was an amateur with money. Variations on this theme recur and it is common practice to make the raising of money a sort of yardstick measuring one's interest. A producer holding a play option, for example, may need better access to funds than he himself possesses. In these circumstances he may negotiate an arrangement along these lines with somebody with richer friends:

1. If by a fixed date you raise at least X percent of the capitalization, your share of my producer's net profits is Y percent, you are to receive billing credit "in association with" after my name, and you and I will jointly make business decisions except that I reserve the right solely to determine when the play is to be closed or abandoned.

2. If by that date you raise less than X percent but at least Y percent, you receive neither billing credit nor joint control but merely Z percent of my producer's net profits.

3. Failing even that, you get nothing but recoupment of expenses approved by me in advance.

Often the newcomer will be needed more to provide "front money" than any substantial part of the ultimate capitalization. What he is most likely to get back for this is recoupment plus a share of the producer's net profits. This kind of negotiation is not necessary at the top rank, but the top rank is small.

Recapitulating briefly, contract patterns in the theatre add up to a Maginot Line protecting the creative artist. What most frequently breaks it is economic reality, not the negotiation of different terms. So unique is the author's position, at least among the performance media, that his agent is the one likely to submit a form contract to the producer instead of the other way around. Famous directors and choreographers (whose work may be a form of literary property) do the same thing. In television or motion pictures this approach is unthinkable. There the merchant, not the creator, has the last word.

Will the theatre remain chaste? That depends on the outcome of two opposite tendencies.

One tendency is decentralization coupled with subsidy, all of which makes for more art and less commerce. National theatres, foundations and repertories are likely to go the artists' way. The barriers may be political rather than commercial as the theatre becomes an ideological laboratory.

The opposite tendency is shaped by the growth of recording techniques. People with cameras are not going to let the theatre alone. Regardless of union problems there is bound to be greater mingling among the performing arts, with videotape and film occasionally taking the place of touring companies, and live television flashing performance direct from the stage across continents and seas. When this happens the new breed will move in.

The new breed are lawyers and business people sophisticated in rights dealings. The most sophisticated among them will have television backgrounds. Their influence will be anti-author, not out of insensitivity but as the result of pragmatism. It will be their point of view that gypsies cannot run industry.

There is no way of telling which tendency will be more apparent over a period of time. I should think each will make considerable impact in its own way. Actually there is no reason why they may not partially be reconciled.

Reconciliation will be effected only by professionals. If the play's the thing, and we are going to have exciting new theatre groups not always obsessed with money, there is no reason for leaving the business end of it to refugees from the campus and garden club. Shakespeare was hard-nosed, and that was a good thing. Sentimentality all too often is either a sword for knaves or at best a shield for dullards.

Even the theatre can reflect order and fair play.

MOTION PICTURES

4

A FILM SALE IS THE GRAND PRIX FOR MANY OWNERS OF literary property. While the theatre is more likely to provide an annuity, the motion picture industry is notable for more immediate reward. Here are some prices from a *New York Times* report of January 26, 1966:

MY FAIR LADY—$5,500,000 cash plus 47½ percent of gross receipts over $20,000,000

SOUTH PACIFIC—$2,270,000

CAMELOT—$2,000,000 plus a percentage of receipts

GUYS AND DOLLS—Over $1,000,000

OKLAHOMA—Over $1,000,000

LIFE WITH FATHER—Over $1,000,000

HAWAII—$600,000 against 10 percent of gross

WANDERERS EASTWARD, WANDERERS WEST—$500,000 plus a percentage of gross

GONE WITH THE WIND—$50,000

The list affords plays a clear edge over books, but it contains only members of the royal family and is therefore unrepresentative in many respects.

75

With high production costs and relatively few products, the motion picture industry plans everything for the long pull. Television has become almost as much concerned with prospective mileage but its original tradition is live—on the air and then on to the next thing. Motion picture tradition is better rooted in world markets. Film rights are, therefore, the most technical of all. Everything must be just so; if a thing can be said one way it can just as easily be said five ways to make sure that management will have everything it requires. In this field the ideal background is part copyright professor and part Prussian. Extemporization is not applauded; you must go by the book. The contract is a feature production.

About background there is little to say which has not become legend. Properties such as books and novels frequently are bought—if not pre-sold—for considerable sums. In some cases the title may be the real thing of value, but whatever induces the purchase it will be books and plays that make the biggest stir when film rights are acquired. Original screenplays bring rewards of their own and are more appropriately discussed in connection with services.

The Establishment penultimately consists of the "major" financier-distributors, ultimately of the banks. Films have been made by private subscription, as in theatrical practice, but summit transactions are done by the Establishment working through independent próduction companies.

Picture companies print up enormous form contracts which they dislike changing. With all the stress on technicalities in this field there is often little to be negotiated unless the Owner is in a strong position. Elaborate and brisk exchanges are catalogued in what follows but they do not occur as a matter of course. That this is true of all media, in fact true of life generally, is no reason to give up underscoring the point. It may be *especially* true in the motion picture field. Assume that the Owner is leading from strength in the discussion that follows.

Plunging at once into icy and uncongenial waters, we find that warranties have all the dark flavor of the Inquisition.

Essentially, different contracts concur, requiring the Owner to give and back up these assurances:

He has sole, unlimited and unencumbered motion picture rights throughout the world.

He has sole authority to grant the rights he is granting.

Everything he grants will be exclusive to the User.

No part of the literary property is in the public domain.

The whole of it except the title may be copyrighted everywhere.

The title in its turn may be used exclusively by the User.

The property is original with its author.

It is devoid of matter violating somebody else's copyrights, right of privacy or other rights, and is not defamatory of anyone.

The Owner has not previously granted the same rights to anybody else or in any other way diminished their scope.

There are no prior copyrights except those listed, and in all prior grants the Owner reserved the right to do what he is doing now.

There are no claims or litigation adversely affecting the property.

No motion picture, television, dramatic or other version has been made and no publication effected, except as listed.

The Owner will not in future make any conflicting grants or otherwise impair the value of what he is selling.

The Owner will not make competitive uses of his reserved rights, if any.

The Owner will hold harmless and indemnify the User, i.e., his purchaser, and everyone claiming through the latter, in respect of the foregoing.

The Owner grants the User the right to sue for infringement of the property.

The Owner will prevent the property and all revisions and new versions of it from going into the public domain, affixing proper copyright notices, executing the right papers, requiring the right moves on the part of his other licensees, and generally behaving as a meticulous if not haunted person.

The Owner agrees finally that if he fails to do any of these things, his purchaser may step in and do it himself, in the Owner's name if necessary.

I have taken the liberty of paraphrasing the usual warranty clauses but the discerning reader, if he has waded through any of this, must have noted certain redundancies in the flow of thought. Still, these are the facts of life when expensive assets are changing hands. Furthermore, it can get stickier.

One film sale document involving a Trust required these further assurances:

A copy of the Trust agreement annexed for all to see.

A copy of the assignment putting the literary property into the Trust.

A book publisher's disclaimer to show that the publisher consents to the film sale and has been "cleared."

Since the individual trustee refuses to undertake personal liability, the author's widow and children swear separately that the rights have been appropriately transferred, and make further pledges.

Then follows the usual division of responsibility which we have seen elsewhere. The Trust warrants nothing with respect to material not in the original version—a book in this case.

In this medium too, you will find on occasion that the seller's liability for breach of warranty is limited to the price he receives, or twice that amount, but, in any case, a fixed percentage. This is not always the case and even when it happens the Owner undertakes huge responsibilities; if nothing else, he pays tax on the amount received, and thus has less than the full amount to pay back if his chain of title is wrong.

Once again, the buyer will want to inspect underlying rights documents. If these prove defective, the Owner will be sent back with instructions to clean everything up. To accomplish this, the Owner will undoubtedly have to pay something additional, if he got rights from somebody else, and there lies the moral of this entire section. The chain of title must be impeccable before one can give all these warranties. This leads directly into the scope of rights.

For all its vital importance the rights grant is less imaginatively treated in motion picture sales than in television, where more unorthodox rights arise. The dead hand of tradition has shaped something that sounds like an insurance policy. Nevertheless there are changes afoot as film companies move into the television business. Broadcasting concepts have reached the old guard and are making an impression. Soon this may be true in all media of communication and the rights grants will become increasingly complex.

Here is a compendium of rights granted culled from the sale of film rights in one straight play, two musicals, one novel and a short story. In the transfer of theatre properties the Dramatists Guild negotiator took part in the negotiations.

The best way to begin is to outline what the motion picture company asks for.

The Owner is to grant (directly or subject to an option) exclusively all motion picture rights including sound, musical and talking motion picture rights now or hereafter known throughout the world, in the literary property and all its component parts, forever. This would include:

Use of the title in conjunction with or apart from the photoplay;

The right to make, exhibit, market and publicize everywhere motion pictures [*sic*] of the property including reissues and remakes, continuations and sequels, air and screen trailers, sound records and stills, with copyright in the purchaser's name;

The right to make changes in everything from characters and themes to the title itself, to modify, translate, add to and take from the property, set it to music and issue sound recordings;

The right to publish in any form including not only excerpts but novelizations;

The right to exploit commercial tie-ups and merchandising;

The right to exhibit the photoplay on any sort of television and to make a television series out of the basic property.

A copyright assignment accompanies this grant, and then there is usually a restriction on rights which the Owner reserves. With formulas of this kind the Owner is lucky to reserve anything at all except what he might have previously granted to others, but theatrical stage rights, for example, may be left in his hands if he promises not to do a play based on the property for a period of years that the parties negotiate. Seven years from the date of release of the first motion picture or ten years from the date of the contract (whichever is later) is a typical formula. Even then the film buyer usually has a first refusal on the rights that were reserved.

More and more as companies diversify they are taking up stage rights as well. Brisk negotiation may spring them loose, but with television the Owner is not likely to get anywhere holding things back. Motion picture companies are in television to stay. They want everything; only the price is negotiable.

Nevertheless there is a curious body of trade practice that hangs on, although diminishingly, and is worth considering as an example of history's workings in this field. I refer to the division of television rights that would have been typical several years before and after 1960.

Early television was partly "live," and videotape, which was shot straight from the floor as the actors performed, kept much of the spontaneous live quality. Film, with its starting and stopping, was a different sort of technique. A practice arose of negotiating ancillary television rights in connection with motion picture sales so as to reflect each of three categories. The Owner reserved live television rights subject to the restrictions and first refusal mentioned in connection with stage rights. The motion picture company acquired film television rights, still with reference to the property itself. Videotape uses actually were cut so fine that often taping in the live manner (direct capture) was reserved to the Owner while taping in the film manner (starting and stopping) went to his purchaser. Series rights generally were withheld by the Owner. At that time people were talking about the one basic work.

In addition, the film company would have the right to do limited television excerpts live for the purpose of advertising its picture, ten to fifteen minutes in the United States and forty minutes in the United Kingdom. Successful playowners were able to restrict exercise of these rights (together with release of the picture itself) sufficiently to avoid competition with the play if it still happened to be running.

Pay-television rights generally were held back completely.

These earlier formulas are of more than historical interest to the rights dealer. Any swingover period suggests lessons useful on the playing field as well as in the library.

I think the points here are at least two.

First, new techniques of communication require the most elaborate division of rights as existing categories become blurred.

Second, as the new techniques become established they are likely to force diversification by companies previously doing only one thing or the other, with the result that fewer rights can be held back generally and the question of price looms even larger since there is no second chance except for reversion. It becomes harder and harder to restrict the scope of the rights transferred but one can still get his rights back if the buyer does nothing within a fixed period of time. Short options may be the answer.

If the last part of this discussion overly reflects the Owner's viewpoint, it must be brought out that the Owner was considered an author. For an author the California practice of asking for everything one can get under the copyright laws is disagreeably unlike New York practice in the theatre. Not every Owner, though, is the writer himself.

The entrepreneur who buys rights for resale must do

things as they are done on the West Coast. Typically, he may be the new breed of author-producer seeking multiple credits. He finds an interesting little novel by an obscure Welshman; he has some vague notion of doing it into a screenplay himself; in any event he wants to lay it off on an independent producer tied in with one of the majors. Sooner or later the rolling stone comes to rest, and it had better be shaped for California. Specifically, in his contract with the author he must acquire enough rights to please Hollywood. Using a studio form may be a good beginning, but only a beginning. Thus, warranties and rights have to be parallel and soundly based.

The third category in this complex medium is services. It may be of some interest here to examine the structure of a rare multiple-picture deal. There is a little bit of everything in it, rights and services together, making a complete manual all its own.

The first document is a letter employing the writer to render his services almost exclusively in writing and/or adapting (there the underlying rights theme is first sounded) five screenplays based on material assigned by the company. The overall work period is five years. During the term of the agreement the writer will not write screenplays designed initially for release in theatres or on pay-television for any-one else, and the remaining projects permitted him will be subordinate to this one. Mutual pledges of cooperation conclude this passage.

The term of employment covering each screenplay is said to commence on a date designated by the company on thirty days' advance written notice. If the writer is ill at the time, he loses only the particular picture, not all five—a point heavily negotiated.

The writer agrees that with each picture he will execute a paper in the form of Contract I annexed or Contract II annexed, whichever is applicable.

If the writer initiates and submits an original story in

the form of a completed screenplay the company has thirty days to elect purchasing all rights for $150,000, including revisions. If they do so elect, another annexed document—Exhibit C (an assignment)—takes effect and one of the five writing projects is deemed consummated. The $150,000 is treated as an advance against profits.

If the company should decline this story and screenplay, then the writer may dispose of them elsewhere. If he does so, the company, even by re-entering the fray after the time limit expires and buying it up on second thought, owes the writer five projects or any balance remaining at the time.

If the writer initiates and submits an original story idea, there is a thirty-day option again, this time to order his writing of a "treatment." Within ten days of delivery of the treatment the company may choose (or not choose) to buy it for $40,000. If it does buy it, the story and treatment become the basis for one of the five projects and the writer must execute another Exhibit C assignment. If it declines, then the writer is free to dispose of this material elsewhere. The company signs an appropriate form of reassignment and gets back half its original payment out of the writer's proceeds from selling the story and treatment elsewhere.

The company gives itself a fourteen-day first refusal right with respect to any novels, plays, musicals and television series as well as original stories and screenplays created by the writer during the term of his employment. Material created earlier is exempt, but has to be listed.

A tax-spreading provision assures the writer that he is not going to be paid more than a specified amount each year even though this device carries the obligation to pay him beyond the five-year term. There can be nothing about segregating these amounts due and holding them in trust because this would spoil the tax saving. The writer must take his chances that the company will remain solvent.

This ends the brief letter agreement and brings one to Contract I. When Contract I takes effect the writer is employed to write a complete first draft screenplay including preliminary material, such as step outlines. The writer's services are exclusive as soon as he is actually at work on one of the five projects. A timetable is set forth and the writer is guaranteed $100,000 if he does what he is supposed to do. Schedule I (not to be confused with Exhibit C or one's insurance policies) then sets out various times for payment:

$10,000 on commencement of employment
$10,000 on delivery of forty-five pages of the first draft screenplay
$10,000 on delivery of ninety pages
$30,000 on delivery of first draft screenplay
$10,000 on expiration of third week after the commencement of revisions
$10,000 on expiration of sixth week after the commencement of revisions
$20,000 on delivery of first draft screenplay incorporating changes

Alternatively, these salaries may be paid at a fixed weekly rate.

Returning to Contract I, there is a good deal of "boilerplate" about illness, getting an injunction if the writer tries to run off somewhere, and complete ownership of his material (backed up by another annexed form and a certificate incorporated directly into the text). Further, the writer gets $500 a week toward living expenses while working in California on this project, and there is a new sort of favorable profits clause.

If the writer is entitled to sole or first joint screenplay credit on the main title, he gets 2½ percent of distributor's gross proceeds. If he is entitled to credit on the main title in some other way, he gets 1¼ percent of distributor's gross proceeds. This compensation is contingent; the amounts firmly committed (mentioned earlier) are deemed an advance against these additional shares.

The inevitable Exhibit "A" defines distributor's gross

proceeds. "Gross proceeds" means all monies derived by the company or any of its subsidiaries from the rental, license, lease, sale or other use of the particular photoplay by anyone, excluding remakes and sequels. "Billings" means rentals, license fees, royalties or other charges billed for the right to exhibit the photoplay except on television. "Television income" means just what you would suppose it means.

Gross proceeds are the aggregate of:

All billings and television income of the company, its subsidiaries, and various listed licenses or substitute distributors in specified countries;

All billings of the company's United States licensee for the photoplay;

Net monies remaining or losses resulting after payment of all expenses from road show engagements;

Net sums from outright sales;

Net sums remitted or paid in the United States by other distributors;

Sums derived from sale of prints less expenses;

Net sums received from settlement or judgment of infringement claims;

Net sums received in settlement of breach claims against exhibitors; and

Net sums received from licensing trailers of the photoplay in the United States.

(Admission receipts of theatres and other items such as merchandising are excluded.)

These gross receipts are to be available for distribution if paid in United States dollars, or if payable in foreign currencies under specified circumstances.

The company may further deduct:

Various taxes on gross receipts and remittances;

Direct cost of checking percentage film engagements of the photoplay;

Freight and other shipping and censorship charges not otherwise reimbursed;

Distribution, synchronization, recording or performing royalties;

Trade association dues and fees;
Foreign quota losses, apportioned;
Payments made in settlement of specified claims.

What remains after these deductions constitutes "distributor's gross proceeds" for the photoplay. The writer's percentage is computed in accordance with these formulas. If the company assigns all its rights in the photoplay, its assignee can recoup the purchase price as an additional deduction. Whether this is fair or not is open to question.

For remakes and sequels there are to be more cash and more percentages. The latter become somewhat detailed and make use of decimal points, but they vary again to reflect billing credit, which in turn reflects how much of the writer's creation has actually been used. All cash payments are advances against percentage points here.

Finally, Exhibit X is tacked on at the end of Contract I. Exhibit X is the Guild rules on billing credit.

Contract II employs the writer to create a treatment in circumstances where the writer has initiated a story idea. It covers much of the same ground, but has a television series rider negotiated in such a way as to reflect trade practice.

If the company does a series based on one or more of the characters—note, "one or more" is better wording for the writer than "characters," where at least two of his brain-children would have to be used before he got the agreed royalties—he gets $500 per new episode and $140 per rerun for a half-hour series; $1,000 and $280 for an hour; $1,500 and $420 for ninety minutes; and $2,500 and $700 for two hours, with billing credit in each case.

Payment and billing credit are related insofar as the screenwriter is concerned. Screen credits generally depend on Guild formulas except where the basic property is adapted from another medium such as a short story. A problem may arise in connection with paid ads. The original author wants his name in all advertising and promotion issued by the company, and perhaps also in that under the company's control, no matter who issues it. The company can go just so far; advertisements can carry only so many names.

Another credit struggle sometimes occurs when a rights owner wants his name on the screen but is not going to do the screenplay. He may negotiate for some different kind of credit like "Associate Producer." This means that he actually is employed as Associate Producer because he can always be laid off under a pay-or-play clause, although next there may be trouble with his successor actually performing that function. One way or another he creates problems.

Control is rarely a question with motion pictures. Artistically and commercially the User has a free hand. Playwrights nourished in the theatre find the terms in film-making very different.

Assignment rights may be more complicated. Sellers to independent producers frequently stipulate that assignment may be made only to one of the majors, not to some other independent producer. Even if a major distributor-financier is on the other end of the contract from the start, there may still be negotiation to restrict brokering, or at least to share any profit on resale. Then too, whatever the law might be otherwise, clauses are added to ensure that the original buyer remains liable if his assignee defaults.

Thus far we have been examining standard sales patterns involving rights and services on the top rank. The game is highly professional, sleek with uniforms cut from the same California cloth.

One example of a contract still largely in the traditional style, but with a touch of television thinking, concerns a comic detective novel. The television clauses themselves are handled traditionally: the purchaser's rights to televise the property itself as distinct from a motion picture based on the property is put on a first refusal basis, together with stage rights. Whether or not the purchaser exercises first refusal rights, the author agrees not to dispose of television or stage rights in the property for ten years from the date of the agreement or seven years from the date of release of any first film made under it, whichever is later, New, however, is the clause giving the purchaser an option—not first refusal, but a true option at an agreed price—to acquire the same motion picture and allied rights in the author's next work using the same detective character. Successive films about the same characters are nothing new, but this sort of option is something of a departure. Authors who dislike the trend must write tragedies in which everyone is killed off.

Rights in all the communications media link together nowadays, especially when performance originates on film. The same company that makes features will produce television shows. It will require not only the right to exhibit its features on television, but the right to present one or more programs based on the underlying literary work by means of television. There is bound to be more and more crisscrossing when rights are sold. A company making features will want the right to release them initially on television. A company that produces television series will want the right to release them in theatres, sometimes in the form of several episodes combined. Unused footage becomes a matter of great concern in these circumstances. New material interpolated by anyone becomes the subject of negotiation. Remember too, all of the rights mentioned are almost certainly bound to be exclusive. Whoever captures them brings home not merely a link, but the whole chain.

How far this can go is not easily foreseen. All of the modern trappings cannot disguise a reversion to older times when authors got very little besides immortality. In 1667 John Milton assigned *Paradise Lost* outright to Tonson's publishing firm in London. Are today's practices much different? Page after page of exhibits spelling out television and sound track rights differ only in form. We may be witnessing old dances with new names.

As against that, Users can point out a number of real

differences. Payments to authors can be astronomical nowadays, and that makes all the difference. Production costs, even abroad, require that the product be exploited in the maximum degree possible. Further, not many authors are like Milton. Many of them offer little more than a device or idea; they are overpoweringly represented by agents and lawyers; and many a rights owner is not the author at all, merely a speculator.

Since logic is less persuasive than power, these questions will be answered in the arena. The West Coast "All the rights you can pay for" philosophy is so fundamentally at variance with the "author knows best" viewpoint best reflected in the theatre that collision is nearly certain. Any new medium is a new battleground for the fundamental control of rights.

One solution we may see more and more is the author joining the other side. Cooperative author projects tend to fall apart because too many strong personalities are involved, but the author-producer in one business form or another is here to stay.

Meanwhile there are plenty of peaceful compromises that keep things going. An amusing one that comes to mind concerned a substantial rights owner who controlled a variety of children's classics. She was selling motion picture and television rights to one of the more successful Hollywood buyers who had a hand in everything. As things went along it struck me that she had reason to be concerned about "image" since there was no telling what film people would do to her precious characters. I asked her for some objective standard we might run into the contract, since continuing approval rights would be out of the question.

Then she sent me a favorite clause which her firm had used once before. It was pretty much what one might expect, and went something like this:

No character in the novels may be shown using alcohol, tobacco, firearms, narcotics or vile language.

Somewhat apprehensively I conveyed this to California, where the buyer surprised me by accepting it. The next day my rights owner, always most engaging in manner, proposed a change in the quoted language that would render it more suitable. She had us make the final period a comma, adding the phrase, "except villains and bullies."

This sort of objective standard serves as a modified form of artistic control. It serves too, as a reminder that there are still standards left.

This concludes consideration of rights patterns in the performance media. There are other media such as radio and live opera but literary property dealing in these media nowadays simply is not much of an industry. A news analyst doing radio tapes for syndication will be concerned with familiar themes: guarantees against profits, reservation of the right to publish, a better contract if an option for television is exercised. The creator of operas may have even less to worry about. Something like art for art's sake will be the essence of his contract in most cases.

Motion pictures offer more tangible rewards. As the industry draws closer to broadcasting, new literary rights patterns are sure to emerge. Still the familiar points will be raised each time; the scope of rights will need meticulous definition, warranties will bristle more formidably than ever, and net profits will be filled with new traps for the unwary.

A different kind of use, though, heralds a real change. I mean education as distinct from divertissement—a difference most notable in publishing.

PUBLISHING

THE PRODUCTION AND DISTRIBUTION OF BOOKS IS NO SIMPLE process, and yet business arrangements in this field are quite different from those in performance media. Victorian is a word that comes to mind, or Edwardian perhaps; there is a more serene atmosphere, and the rules of the game are simpler. We leave grandmaster chess for the more innocent delights of double solitaire.

Publishing contracts are simpler for a number of reasons. Tradition is one, but the smaller amounts of money at stake afford a truer (if less delicate) explanation. The magnitude of the battle is consequently diminished, although agents do sometimes obtain "motion picture figures" for books. Perhaps most significant is the absence of lawyers from most encounters, something far different from the usual television or film sale where counsel for the author and counsel for his agency meet week after week with counsel for the producer and counsel for the producer's financiers, with various managers, accountants and other representatives poking the coals whenever they burn low. This omission in arranging most book contracts is noteworthy.

And a good thing too, many people would say, because the line suggests itself almost inevitably, as platitudes so often do. A moment's reflection, however, dispels the euphoria created by images of two grey-haired kindly men smoking pipes and settling everything in a civilized way.

Probably the contract for a book will be negotiated directly by the author, or by his agent, with the publisher, or with one of his editors, using a printed form drawn up a decade earlier by the publisher's lawyer who has long since retired to raise sheep. The parties agree that television rights are to be split 10 percent to the publisher, 90 percent to the author, or whatever. There it all is, with no fuss.

But *what* television rights? Special or series, or both together? Is a character spin-off to be shared with the publisher? What if series segments are merged and released as a theatrical film? Probably such points will never be raised. Ultimately, the absence of lawyers may mean everybody has to go to court. The best that over-simplification generally accomplishes is the use of a barrister instead of a solicitor.

The position is even more unpleasant when publishers have the right to sell subsidiary rights and then divide proceeds with their authors. Fortunately this practice is infrequent since only the most exceptional publisher will have found leisure to become expert in the fields of television, the theatre and motion pictures. At any rate, it is unlikely to survive very much longer. Developments in the craft of publishing and the dissemination of information generally are so spectacular that the gentle dowager lady soon may be leading the commandos.

Publishing is an ancient industry. In *The World of Books in Classical Antiquity* (Leiden, 1958), the late Dr. H. L. Pinner gives us this sample of Roman commerce:

Publishing concerns soon showed signs of organized manufacture. In order to be able to deal with the work of reproduction quickly and on a large scale, the publishers kept a specially trained staff. For this job slaves were employed, usually Greeks as far as we can judge from names known to us. They were much sought after and expensive. A whole staff of such copyists represented a considerable capital outlay. Horace directs his wit at the prices paid by connoisseurs for slaves who 'have a smattering of Greek.' According to Seneca 100,000 sesterces (about £1,000 gold) used to be paid for a '*servus literatus*.' Slaves were even educated as calligraphers from childhood. Though enslaved, they were paid for their work. Wages were, however, low, especially under the early emperors. Later on, the rates of pay were better. The Emperor Diocletian in an edict fixes the maximum price for 100 lines of the finest writing at 25 denarii (5½ gold pence); for a lower standard the rate was 20 denarii. Female slaves were also said to be experienced and skilful copyists, just as women today have proved their worth as compositors. . . . A well organized publishing firm could in a few days put on the market hundreds of copies of a new book.

Hundreds of years ago, Tonson's publishing house in London owned *Paradise Lost* and were considered to own Shakespeare's copyrights. Thus publishing is an ancient as well as a formidable business whose outmoded treatment of literary property is all out of accord with its importance.

Let us consider what has been happening since World War II. The so-called paperback revolution is what most people would mention first, but other developments are just as impressive. Publishing-house mergers and public investment, the proliferation of book clubs and selling by mail generally, the decline of bookshops and the development of new outlets like supermarkets have made vast changes. While the apparatus has grown, the subject matter has proliferated equally and English has become the world's second language. Hardcover adult "trade" books have come to account for less than a tenth of industry product. More textbooks and stronger university presses reflect a world that demands information if not wisdom.

The Times Literary Supplement (London) of September 30, 1965 ran an article called "The Heavy Industry of Writing." The article itself is a first-class sample of British writing and its title is peculiarly well suited to the subject. It quotes Hans Magnus Enzensberger, a German author, as saying, "The consciousness industry is bound to perpetuate the existing power structure," and takes note of a trend by which I suppose many authors would like being engulfed:

A new market, new distribution channels, a new industrial scale for the publishing business. Anyone who has followed the Frankfurt Book Fair each autumn knows what has happened in the past few years. We have seen something like a rapid development from artisan production to heavy industry. In the course of becoming industrialized publishing firms have come to make new demands on the author. In the old days, the author used to plan his book at leisure, then offer it to the publisher. Nowadays the publisher commissions the book from the author; he wants a book a year from him, or even one every six months, forcing his imagination into a given rhythm that has to correspond to the rhythm of the market. This phenomenon, already familiar in big American publishing firms, is now spreading to areas which have long remained artisanal: two years ago we saw the first instance of an Italian publisher giving a young poet a regular income in exchange for first rights on all his work. This was not a novelist, but a poet, and a young and difficult one.

Actually I know someone who commissions books, then sells them as a package to large publishing houses. Distributing through others and retaining an interest in the proceeds sounds familiar enough to anyone who has done television. Once again we see different media coming together in production concept.

Further development may lead to initial publication in paperback instead of hardback, and over-all contracts with authors that include paperback and hardcover rights. The real explosion has taken place already, in the growing series of contacts between publishers and the electronics industry. Early partnerships talked about in the book industry were between Raytheon and Heath, Xerox and Wesleyan University Press, RCA and Random House. I use "partnerships" in the Pickwickian sense. Whatever the internal arrangements, the results are incalculable.

The entire learning process will be affected. Audiovisual aids may become more than aids, and supplant reading. Push-button information retrieval (raising a new host of copyright problems) is becoming standard procedure. Inexpensive copying has made it possible for schools and foundations to publish their own material. I should not be surprised to find IBM and Xerox awarding academic degrees. The future of books is uncertain; the future of people is even more so.

These visionary projections round out our picture of the Establishment in this last major medium. There is irony in the picture: you find oversimplified and old-fashioned contract arrangements governing events even more radical than the invention of broadcasting. Soon it must all change.

Thus far, however, there has been relatively little in the way of contract apocalypse. One indication of forward motion was the change in the fifty-fifty split of income from paperback reprints announced by W. W. Norton & Co. It made quite a splash in writing circles, and I recall articles in various trade magazines as well as cheery lectures offered by one or two authors' societies when the news was announced. Norton was reported offering authors 50 percent of the first $10,000 of paperback revenue collected; 55 percent of the next $15,000; 60 percent of the next $75,000; 65 percent of the next $150,000; and 75 percent thereafter. Changes of this kind certainly are significant but they have the sound of dulcimers when a trumpet voluntary would be more fitting.

Let us now consider the forms of book contracts still in use today. A preliminary point is that arrangements vary sharply depending on the number and quality of contributors. For example, an expensive book with important illustrations is unlikely to bring an author his normal royalty share. The cost of the pictures simply is not going to be borne solely by the publisher. Similarly, a compendium sets its own ground rules. Twice I have had articles taken by publications where multiple contributors were being paid according to some proportionate scale. The first time it was a Dutch law encyclopedia that paid by the page. Since I had contributed only three pages, the remuneration was modest, and my wife suggested that I should write to Holland and ask them to send me a cheese. The second time it was a collection of articles about Sherlock Holmes. Here we divided a 20 percent royalty according to the number of contributors. That a loaf can be sliced in so many ways suggests an interesting parallel between scribbler and panifact.

Contributions to magazines and newspapers are less likely to be paid pro rata. For our purposes, these media will not be considered part of "the heavy industry of writing" because they do not engage large numbers of professional service people in negotiating complex sales of literary property. Nevertheless, it is worth mentioning that besides flat payment the contributor usually can expect assignment back to himself of those non-periodical rights which the magazine will not need for its own use. Syndicated articles require more elaborate agreements, but anyone familiar with options and guarantees and related concepts dealt with earlier in this book should have no trouble working things out, or at least knowing what has to be covered.

Returning to our main theme, book contract negotiations (what there are of them) encompass our seven basic points.

Warranties in this medium are reasonably simple. Cross-indemnities by the publisher are infrequent since this is one field in which Users do not ordinarily interpolate material.

That there are no actors depicting named persons may be another distinction that diminishes risk in some jurisdictions. Legal distinctions of this kind may become interesting with biographies, but the law is unsettled. This may be something to keep in mind when you are dealing with the printed equivalent of "documentaries."

Insurance may be one way out of a deadlock over risky books. I know at least one instance where the publisher paid premiums, but the creators were top names. Usually the author must hold his publisher harmless. More likely than not he will be without resources to do so, and the publisher will be sued as well. Still the warranty clause is seen everywhere. Possibly it reminds authors to take care.

The Rights point is more open to negotiation. Time and space, typically, are key considerations. Generally, a formula brings the two together. The author says, "I will grant the right to do this, that and the other but it reverts to me if you fail to do it within the agreed time." More specifically, the publisher may acquire something along these lines:

1. Exclusive book rights in English in the United States and Canada and the Philippines or other imperial remnants with non-exclusive rights to export elsewhere. In this category there may be no stated time limit, although in some cases the author has recaptured his rights in court.

2. Exclusive rights to license publication throughout the British Commonwealth, except Canada, revocable if no such arrangement has been concluded within eighteen months after American publication.

3. Exclusive rights to license publication elsewhere in all other languages, revocable country by country or language by language on a similar basis, except that the time limit is three years.

Subsidiary rights generally divide into two categories: print media and performance media. In the first category would be the normal adjuncts of publishing, such as serialization rights, book-club rights, reprints and paperbacks, digests and microfilming. In the second would be television, radio, motion pictures, phonograph recordings, and legitimate stage rights. Usually the publisher controls those in the first category.

Some publishers take almost all book rights including copyright in their own name. At the other end of the spectrum you may find a London publisher taking only the right to publish in Great Britain and Northern Ireland, while if an Authors Guild recommendation were to be followed in America, the publisher would have only the United States and Canada. Sometimes literary agents are in a bargaining position to hold back even foreign and first serial rights.

Geography is not easily obscured, but time questions and the vitality of affirmative obligations are not all that simple. Many publishing contracts obscure both. Publishers come astonishingly close to a "must publish" clause, subject to delays occasioned by *force majeure* and to rejection of certain material. In the other fields we have considered, this sort of commitment would be unthinkable. Actually agree to put on a play? Commit to finish and release a film? Only the rankest amateur would fall into that sort of trap. Management protects itself all the way by continuing options and escape clauses. As against that, there are publishing contracts by whose terms the failure to publish would be breach of contract. Even if publication is not enforced, there may be damages for breach.

On the other hand, publishers often acquire options on next books. Through this device, publishers go one step beyond many producers in making tough bargains. Their idea is to pre-empt an author's next work, but it must be done skillfully. Nearly always it is done amateurishly. Most of the option clauses in book contracts are so vague as to be incomprehensible if not actually unenforceable. Some of them translate into first refusals, not options. Hard line or soft line, you cannot always tell them apart. This is all very well, assuming people understand generalities and will behave like gentlemen, but I see nothing wrong in assisting the process by clear rules. Either somebody must publish a book or he need not, provided that such and such will happen if he decides not to. Either he has a clear option with time limits and machinery for furnishing notice, or he has something else, or he has nothing. Lay it all out in advance. Experience demonstrates that people are more likely to be ladies and gentlemen under compulsion. Good contracts make good partners.

The grant of rights usually is terminable, with an author's option to buy plates and remaining copies at discount prices if the publisher fails to keep the work in print and for sale. This is reminiscent of theatre practice.

Writers' services fit uneasily into this chapter. Writers of books are not unionized, and so the distinction between rights and services that becomes perilously blurred elsewhere is not yet a factor. This is not to suggest that authors lack organized spokesmen. Actually the most useful guide to book contracts from the author's viewpoint that I have seen has been issued by the Authors Guild.

It would be a mistake, however, to assume that authors never will be employees. The electronics era may turn more and more of them into industry drones writing up technical data. When this happens, unions will follow. Even now there are writers hired to write books from ideas by the publisher. Generally, staff people retain little right to do anything with their creations, even to share proceeds from subsequent sales. On the other hand, their terms of employment are the subject of negotiation. It may be that creative services will become in the book field what they became early in motion pictures and television. One may only hope that a few eccentric spirits will remain free lance.

Payment comes mainly in the form of royalties. There is everything from flat fees to copublication profit splits but royalties are standard. Sometimes, as in the multiple-picture contract, an author stipulates that less than the full payment due him in a particular year will be paid when due. This sort of income spreading for legitimate tax savings must be done only on professional advice.

Typical royalties on sales of a regular trade edition would be 10 percent of the retail catalogue price for the first 5,000 copies sold; 12½ percent on the next 5,000; 15 percent on all copies sold over 10,000, less returns in each case and with variations in special circumstances, such as remainder sales. Some authors do better. Others, especially when there are several contributors, will not do as well.

The advance payment against royalties is also standard practice, and a frenetically pleasing one to most authors. Others occasionally eschew advances and take higher royalties instead, spreading the income for tax reasons. Theoretically, advances have to be returned if the manuscript proves unacceptable to the publisher but rarely is this an issue in practice. What it accomplishes is to create further ambiguity concerning the "must publish" commitment. Few advances, however, will be paid in full on signature of the contract. By dividing an advance into installments the publisher can cut his losses if the author turns in a complete botch.

Earlier I mentioned a change in the fifty-fifty paperback formula; to the same effect are a number of protests aimed at the discount provisions. Various contract clauses reduce or abolish royalties when books are sold on the cheap or given away for one reason or another. Some of the reasons appear valid—especially keeping a fading book in print—since manufacturing costs per copy tend to rise when there are small reprintings. New methods of copying, however, will upset much of the economics still taken for granted in publishing books.

Royalties are accountable semiannually in most contracts. Frequently, accounting statements will be unintelligible to authors, but there may be poetic justice in this, since the writings of some authors will be unintelligible to their readers.

Subsidiary rights proceeds may be divided according to any number of formulas. Syndication or second-serial rights and book-club rights may go fifty-fifty. Microfilming and motion picture rights often will be shared equally too, while television and "commercial" (merchandising) rights are likely to go 90 percent to the author and 10 percent to the publisher. There is really no fixed custom and the points are negotiable. All one can say is that everything should be spelled out a little more clearly than is usually done. Television, for example, is by no means a single concept.

As to the basic justice of dividing proceeds, there is much to be said on both sides. Publishers will contend that they are burdened with high costs and that they bring life to fallow property. Authors respond that their works are their own brain children and that publishers ought to share, for example, in film sales only when publishers arrange them. I incline to the authors' side here, but I have never been a publisher.

Control is a sensitive issue in publishing. Creatively, nothing is spelled out in so many words but the author is required to submit a manuscript "in content and form satisfactory to the publisher" within a time limit. Naturally this language or its equivalent creates pressure on all except top level writers. One result is that authors accept a good many suggestions from editors whose qualifications vary. Of course, sometimes the suggestions are valid and accepted with good grace.

Control over the disposition of rights follows no fixed practice. Print medium rights, as noted before, are usually "placed" by the publisher as an adjunct of what he does with books. The performing arts are something else again. Generally, the author reserves these with the hope of sale through his agent. Sometimes the publisher acts as his agent, and occasionally goes further and *controls* motion picture and other performing rights. Control by the publisher is an unpleasant business in my view. Dealings in television, the theatre and motion pictures are complex and specialized, and I know very few publishers with the ability or manpower to negotiate effectively in these areas. Agents and lawyers are better at it, at least some agents and some lawyers.

Billing credit ranks lowest with books. Credit to the author is taken for granted and there is none of the passionate haggling over size and placement that enlivens the theatre and related fields. I should say that billing credit as a publishing point comes up only in special cases. One special case defies all the normal laws of gravity in that the true author provides that he is to get no credit as author, but as collaborator or something less. This is now characteristic of ghost writers ever since several law cases held passing off A's work as B's a fraud on the public. Then too, in the book world, there is greater use of pen names than in other media. Oxford dons who write mysteries find this disguise inordinately congenial.

Assignment tends to be understated in publishing. Reference *en passant* to the publisher's "successors and assigns" is just a little casual when so much is at stake. Admittedly the traditional publisher does not lay off his burdens on distributor-financiers as do most producers, but everything is changing. As the electronic "partner" looms larger, every publisher will want elaborately worded rights to copublish and assign. Every author in turn should be very much on guard or he might find his manuscript published by people and in forms never imagined by anyone.

Without rejoicing at the advent of electronic brain-washing, one must still deal with it. A great deal of creative thought is called for. I recommend television patterns as the most fruitful for study. While not wholly applicable, they suggest rules for walking through mazes.

A closer study of present usage is best made by outlining the useful manual issued by the Authors Guild, together with one or two contracts.

The Guild manual lists the following subjects in a preliminary index:

> Royalty
> Grant
> Termination
> Return of Manuscript
> Delivery of Manuscript and Publication
> Copyright
> Proofreading
> Discounts
> Warranty and Indemnity
> Payment
> Option
> Book Club
> Reprint

Motion Picture Rights
Television Rights
Foreign-Language Rights
Syndication
Commercial Rights
Arbitration
Free Copies

Since the contract for this book is representative, I shall take the liberty of summarizing it.

In the grant clause, the publisher's form contract takes the rights earlier mentioned as typical, three years to arrange foreign deals and all. In this case, the author has negotiated a rider changing the basic grant of rights to publish in English. The grant is now limited to eighteen months after delivery of complete manuscript. A time limit of this duration is more consonant with usage in the performance media.

The warranty clause is normal and the publisher has typed in one additional warranty to the effect that there has been no previous publication of this material. Its prior publication in any form is not to constitute over 50 percent of the work and may not be licensed without the publisher's consent, which means no right to do 50 percent or any other fraction at all.

As is usual now, copyright is in the author's name.

The author agrees to deliver manuscript within two years. It proved possible to turn it in sooner, but there is no use making commitments you never can keep.

The author is made responsible for certain correction costs at the printer's. This raises the alarming prospect of turning money back out of pocket. To soften the severity of this provision, the negotiated rider provides that these costs will be deducted from future royalties.

These royalties are then fixed at the usual 10 percent on the first 5,000; 12½ percent on the next 5,000; 15 percent thereafter. Percentages are based on catalogue retail price on sales of the regular trade edition less returns but with no deductions for bad debts.

In addition, the author receives 5 percent on all copies sold by direct mail; 10 percent of publisher's net on discount copies of 50 percent or more; two-thirds of applicable royalty on annual sales aggregating fewer than 400 copies of the trade edition, if sold from a second printing of not over 2,000 copies; 5 percent for "inexpensive editions" as defined; no royalties on free copies to the author; 10 percent for remainder copies; 75 percent of foreign rights; 50 percent of print medium subsidiaries, which are controlled here by the publisher; 85 percent of performance medium subsidiaries, which are jointly controlled (no matter, there is not very much chance of a film sale); and 75 percent of any one-part version issued before publication. All accountings are semiannual.

The agreed rider provides that all advances are non-returnable. This provision rules out another alarming possibility.

Next follow some boiler-plate clauses dealing with subjects on the Guild list, such as termination and arbitration. Somewhat more interesting are two additional rider provisions authors are only likely to get with professional books. One says that no textual changes will be made by the publisher. The other makes all promotional and jacket material subject to the author's advance reasonable approval qualified by certain objective standards.

You can see that not all of the negotiated changes involve money. Some of them do, but only to prevent out-of-pocket reimbursement; most of the other changes deal with intangibles.

There is one final provision in the rider that I urge everyone to request if he writes constantly on a specialized subject. It makes clear that nothing in this contract debars the author from writing further on the same subject as long as he avoids using the contents of this book in the new publication. This is a point I always find difficulty in wording agreeably to both sides but it should not be omitted.

Finally, with reference to this contract, the option has been struck out.

In the publishing field all of this comes to a fair number of changes. In television, or in the theatre, it would be nothing at all. But there it would not have been equally pleasant.

Now let me take up something a little trickier, with a touch of the new "audio-visual" element. I am looking at a contract for a book about music, supplemented by phonograph recordings. Many of its provisions are similar to those just examined. Nevertheless, the addition of records brings back some of the more theatrical points.

For one thing, there is a clear provision about billing credit on containers and jackets.

For another, there is a division of risk stemming from interpolated material. The publisher is responsible for clearing music and must indemnify the author in this respect.

Finally, the author receives additional monies from sales of the record.

Equally in the modern mode is a university project for publication of a whole series of textbooks. As one of a group of advisers, I suggested that the university retain television series rights based on the courses, together with ownership of any new educational techniques that might emerge from them, insofar as they might be protectable. This suggestion did not go down easily although it was later adopted. First impression was that this kind of theatrical notion never should have been brought in at all. I mention it solely as a sample of publishing "climate." They have got a bear by the tail but keep pretending it is only an old classmate.

Admittedly education is not theatre. Still, many of the same principles apply when you are dealing with literary property and some of the strange new elements that it comprises.

The strangest of all are considered briefly in the final chapter of this book. In an effort to be "practical," we have dwelled too long on the apparatus of communication and the customs of industry. That there is such a thing as being *too* practical is uniquely evident in this field.

Literary property is born of the imagination. A visit to its birthplace may help us to predict its future.

THE CICERO CASE

LITERARY PROPERTY MAY BE CLASSIFIED UNDER THREE HEAD-
ings: Compositions, Insignias and Secrets.

Classification along these lines has to be made without
regard to the custom of any single industry but with attention
to usage in general. Nowadays the frontiers of literary property extend further than is generally supposed, marking a vast
empire troubled by uncertain holdings as if numberless earl-
doms, fiefs, enclaves and satrapies were contiguous, and their
sentries dozed.

Compositions are complete works, self-contained even if
presented together with other works as part of a larger
scheme. In this category would be products of the mind traditionally protected by copyright law, ranging from books,
plays, essays and poems at one end to less creative efforts such
as directories and code books at the other. Compositions are
also compounds consisting of severable elements which may
themselves fall within the second category, Insignias.

Insignias are elements that serve originally as identifying
devices only to become ends in themselves later on. Medieval
guild marks and the old emblems of heraldry turned from
signatures into mercantile assets or collectors' items. The
means became ends and the badge took on value in its own
right, sometimes in a new setting.

So, with elements that compose literary compounds, history appears bound to repeat itself. One character in a novel

may be pulled out and live dozens of lives elsewhere in new stories. He may have been the most valuable thing in the original work but discovery of this point takes a little time. When it happens, his owner may be protected legally by doctrines of unfair competition rather than copyright. Possibly too, new forms of incorporeal property are involved.

Insignias as devices with potential lives of their own can include fictional characters and character names, code numbers, places, eras, races, compositions, schools, organizations, events, doctrines, social classes, sayings, props, even the director's staging interpretation which is spelled out as owned by one side or the other in theatre contracts at the present time. Elements of this kind identify Compositions and their authors, and eventually may dwarf them. For example, if somebody writes, "007 solved the case of Wilson, the notorious canary trainer by recourse to the lost book mentioned by Geoffrey of Monmouth," he uses insignias of Ian Fleming, Conan Doyle and Geoffrey himself if his lost book is a fiction as medievalists believe.

Secrets make up the final category, but here we require a prologue. A subject suited to this prologue is the famous spy episode from World War II known as "Operation Cicero."

The facts (with embellishment) have been publicized in two books, a motion picture, and a television program. "Operation Cicero" took place in Turkey between October, 1943 and April, 1944. Briefly, an Albanian valet to Sir Hughe Knatchbull-Hugessen, the British Ambassador, sold photographs of secret documents in his employer's custody to a German agent named Moyzisch. The valet, known to his Nazi masters only by the code name, "Cicero," was paid off by them in counterfeit bills.

This bitter ending raises an intriguing problem, leaving aside morality and the question whether successive German regimes should be responsible for commitments undertaken by the Third Reich. Just what was Cicero selling? What was the legal consideration for his contract to be paid? The easy answer is that he was rendering services, but there is a lot more in it.

The subject of negotiation and sale here was secret intelligence. The spy simply took pictures and sold them; there was no editing, no evaluation of what the documents contained, none of the usual "annotation" we think of in connection with creating intangible assets out of information as such. It was all risky enough, but not part of the creative process.

Now let us consider the position more closely. If I am coming down Snowdon after a good climb, camera in hand, and I stumble through sheer clumsiness and inadvertently photograph a little Welsh girl holding a kitten, and the resultant picture wins several awards as "snapshot of the year," I really have done nothing except bumble onto a good thing. Still, I have become owner of a valuable asset.

Similarly, if I am forced down by engine trouble in flight over the Soviet Union, and I see new model fighters lined up on the field, something of value is locked in the memory even though subsequently disclosed without compensation to the proper authorities.

In the climbing case there will be a tangible record of an experience, while in the flying case there will be nothing but information. In both cases the "owner" of the resulting asset does nothing notable in acquiring it. On the contrary, he seems plagued by bad luck and is probably accident prone.

Nevertheless if society regards each man as an owner by hook or by crook, Cicero is an owner, and if Cicero is an owner, anyone acquiring secret intelligence honorably owns something too, even more clearly.

That would be how society looks at it: willingness to pay is always a sure sign. The law may have different standards. Ideas as ideas are not susceptible of ownership. Knowing something, or how to do something, is unprotectable too, unless you show abuse of a confidential relationship or a contract.

And yet there are few subjects more deserving of immediate study for the development of new rules. Communication more than ever has the power to rock men's brains. Compositions and Insignias condition us daily; Secrets have even greater potency, and may blast the world. Incorporeal property transcends the hardware that records it.

These notions suggested by the Cicero case are something more than theoretical exercise. Pragmatists dealing in literary property may be aware that legal protection usually depends on some flash of originality, but they never can be quite sure. One element may be more important than the compound. One tribunal may protect that element and name its value. It seems wiser to be prepared than to be cavalier.

Accordingly, the most practical thing is to keep all of these notions in mind even though it may often be unwise to make issues of them. In the theatrical arts, Compositions tend to subdivide into Insignias. Information-gathering engenders different kinds of communication and involves Secrets.

"Operation Cicero" is not the last of its kind. There will be other cases involving order of battle or the configuration of planets, new brain-washing techniques, privately circulated pronouncements of party doctrine. Side by side there will always be traffic in the more benign intangibles traditionally thought of as literary property—the fictional spy's code name borrowed to sell children's assassin kits, and occasionally *Hamlet*.

Literary property constitutes an estate of incalculable value. Whoever deals with it must know how to measure apparitions, and put quicksilver into a mold. If these things are not easy of accomplishment, there is always one consolation: The attempt in itself is a creative act. That makes it worth doing; otherwise we are all apprentices in a new craft.

APPENDIX

NOTE—The following contract forms are used by substantial buyers of literary property. They are submitted here only as samples reflecting existing trade practice. Each of them is incomplete and no better than other contract forms designed for the same purpose. All of them normally will be challenged and negotiated by authors or other rights owners.

What is most important, none of these forms should be used without the advice of competent legal counsel.

Form I is for the acquisition of television series rights in a format. Often, provisions on residuals, profit shares, and billing credit will be added. The free option is intolerable from the owner's viewpoint.

Form II is a dramatization agreement for legitimate stage rights in a novel or other non-theatrical work. The specifics ranging from time limits to percentage of gross weekly box office receipts are treated in a side document. This contract sets out a structure that a manager or producer would find desirable.

Form III is a motion picture and allied rights agreement. Frequently it will become operative only if an option set forth in a preliminary document is exercised. To call it "pro-purchaser" is understatement.

Form IV is a book publication contract. Less one-sided than Forms I, II, or III, it still requires study by any author.

Examples of pro-author forms are not given because generally there is no such thing. Contracts are issued by rights purchasers. Thereafter the position is balanced by negotiation and the addition of new provisions.

Form I

(Company Address)

Gentlemen:

In what follows you and I fully set forth our agreement, which is governed by the laws of New York and may not be changed orally, concerning a certain format and presentation for television provisionally entitled _____ (hereinafter referred to as the "Property") annexed hereto and made part of this agreement by reference.

1. I warrant and represent that as copyright proprietor I solely own and control television rights (as hereinafter defined) in the Property without encumbrance and that the Property is original and free of unlawful matter; and I will hold harmless and indemnify you, your officers, directors, agents, associates, assignees and licensees from and with respect to any and all claims, losses, damages, expenses (including reasonable counsel fees) and other liabilities arising out of or in connection with any breach of the foregoing warranties and/or your use of the Property as permitted hereunder. You will similarly indemnify me with respect to material interpolated by you.

2. In consideration of your payment to me of the sum of One Dollar ($1.00), receipt of which I hereby acknowledge, and of your reasonable efforts to arrange for telecast of a series based on the Property, I hereby grant to you the exclusive and irrevocable option to acquire television rights in the Property. To be effective, your exercise of such option must be manifest by furnishing me with written notice thereof no later than _____, absent which timely option exercise all television rights (less material furnished by you) shall revert to me. Timely notice of option exercise must either (a) be accompanied by payment to me in the amount of $_____ representing an advance against royalties hereinafter specified, or (b) truthfully recite that you have made arrangements for production of a pilot program or series (defined as any minimum order of programs). In the event you elect to and do comply with these requirements for the exercise of your option, I shall be deemed automatically to have granted and you shall acquire television rights in and to the Property.

3. Television rights are defined as the exclusive and perpetual right to effect telecast anywhere and throughout the world live, on tape or film or any recording device now existing or hereafter devised; to obtain copyrights and renewals thereof throughout the world; to alter the Property and effect telecast thereof in any length, form or language, sponsored or unsponsored, with or without interpolated material by others, by means of free, pay, closed circuit, CATV, satellite, over the horizon, black and white or color television, by network, local, regional or syndication exhibition, and in theatres or other places of assembly whether or not admission is charged, singly or combined with other programs, or as part of any series or group of programs and otherwise to effect telecast with advertising and promotion thereof and normal ancillary exploitation such as merchandising, printed synopsis and radio simulcast in all ways now existing or hereafter devised, all with associates and upon terms and conditions solely (as between us) of your designation from time to time; to dispose of, deal in and exploit such rights; and all of the foregoing rights apply and are granted equally with respect to sound tracks of any program hereunder, with respect to the extricable elements of the Property, including without limitation title, plots, format, characters, music and other elements susceptible of separate telecast in a separate "spin-off" series, and with respect to new material connected with the Property.

4. I agree not to exercise any reserved non-television rights in the Property and/or in its component extricable elements until termination of the television broadcasting rights of yourselves and any of your licensees (of which date you will advise me at my written request) plus a period of eighteen (18) months.

5. In the event you exercise the foregoing option and undertake production of a program or series based on the Property we agree that I shall accept as total royalty compensation the following amounts payable within ten (10) days after initial network telecast of each new episode in such series or, if any new episode is not originally given network telecast, within ten (10) days after commencement of each run thereof throughout the world:

a. For half-hour programs, $————————
b. For hour programs, $————————
c. For program episodes of any other length, a royalty pro-rated against (b).

6. Subject to the foregoing royalty arrangements all material and programs in any series based on the Property or on any of its extricable component elements shall, upon your exercise of the option, belong unconditionally and perpetually to you with full rights of as-

signment to anyone and the right to use my name, likeness and biographical data concerning me in connection with the series but not as an endorsement of any product or service. During any network exhibition of the series I will neither endorse nor render services or furnish materials in connection with any program advertising any product or service advertised on the series hereunder. At any time and from time to time you may assign this agreement fully or in part to anyone provided, however, that you shall remain liable for payment thereunder if such assignee defaults.

7. During any first network exhibition of the series I will render services as a consultant for the series on a non-exclusive basis for total salaried compensation in the sum of $——— per new program. Nothing herein obligates you actually to utilize my said services or to undertake or continue production of any series or to compensate me, provided compensation is otherwise due hereunder, with respect to any number of series programs greater than the number for which you have a firm order and are fully paid.

8. While this agreement sets out the material terms and conditions of our agreement I shall, at your request, sign further agreements consonant with normal industry practice including without limitation a morals clause, F. C. C. compliance provision and other stipulations required by your network, sponsor or other licensee.

9. Additional conditions:

Agreed To:
Company
By ————————

Very truly yours,

————————————

FORM II

AGREEMENT made this ———— day of ——————————, 19——, by and between

(hereinafter referred to as "Owner") and

(hereinafter referred to as "Purchaser")

WITNESSETH:

FIRST: The Owner represents, warrants and agrees:

(a) That the Owner is the owner of a certain literary work presently entitled

(hereinafter called the "Work"), the sole author of which is ————
———————————— (hereinafter called the "Author"); that the Work is wholly original with the aforementioned author and has not been copied in whole or in part from any other work; that the Work will be published and/or registered for copyright as set forth in subdivision (1) of the annexed Schedule "A" and has not otherwise been published or registered for copyright; that all copyrights in the Work will be valid, existing and unimpaired and that the Work is not in the public domain anywhere in the world where copyright protection is available for the Work; that the term "Work" as used herein includes also any and all additional material, suggestions and ideas which the Owner may have heretofore furnished or may hereafter furnish to Purchaser or anyone on Purchaser's behalf in connection with the Work or any play adapted therefrom and includes also any and all present and future versions, adaptations and publication of the Work;

(b) Except for the rights to be granted by the Owner in the instruments described in subdivision (1) of the annexed Schedule "A," that the Owner is the sole and exclusive owner throughout the world of all rights of every kind and nature in the Work; that the Owner is free, and has full and exclusive warrant and authority, to make this agreement and grant the rights herein granted; that the Owner has not heretofore granted, sold, assigned, encumbered or otherwise disposed of any right, title or interest in and to the Work; that there is not now outstanding any right, title, interest, claim, contract or commitment in or in connection with the Work similar or adverse to or inconsistent with the rights granted to Purchaser or by which any of such rights or the full enjoyment and exercise thereof by the Purchaser may be diminished, invalidated, impaired or affected; that subdivision _____ of Schedule "A" includes all dispositions of or affecting the Work heretofore made whether or not similar, adverse to or inconsistent herewith.

(c) That the Work does not, and the use of the Work herein authorized will not, infringe upon the copyright of any other work or violate the property or any right of privacy or any other right of any person, firm or corporation, and that there has never been any claim or litigation existing or threatened involving the title, ownership or copyright in the Work or the rights herein granted.

SECOND: The Owner hereby grants, sells, and assigns to the Purchaser, upon the terms and conditions herein stated, the following complete, sole and exclusive rights, absolutely and forever throughout the world and in any and all languages, in the Work, which the Purchaser may exercise or cause, authorize or permit others to exercise:

(a) To dramatize the Work and to make, write and compose one or more dramatic or dramatico-musical plays (hereinafter called the "Play") based upon and utilizing the Work, together with the free and unrestricted right to use, adapt, translate, change, rearrange, interpolate in, transpose, add to and subtract from the Work, its situations, incidents, language, plot, theme, characters, dialogue, title, sets, scenes, costume designs, pantomime, direction, action, business, text, descriptive matter, ideas, names, songs, lyrics, music, or otherwise, all as Purchaser may determine in Purchaser's sole discretion.

(b) To produce and present, or cause to be produced and presented, the Play on the speaking stage.

(c) To own, make, perform, exhibit, produce, reproduce, use, sell, publish, lease, license, encumber, copyright or otherwise dispose of or deal in the Play and any dramatic, motion picture, radio, television or other versions and adaptations thereof, and to exercise all rights therein of every kind and nature now known or hereafter ascertained for any and all purposes and by any and all means.

(d) To select and contract with one or more dramatists, adapters, and, if the Play be a musical play, with one or more bookwriters, composers and lyricists, and with any other authors (all hereinafter collectively referred to as the "Dramatists") to prepare the Play, as the Purchaser may determine in Purchaser's sole discretion.

THIRD: In full consideration for the Owner's representations, warranties and agreements herein and the rights granted hereunder, the Purchaser agrees to pay to Owner, and Owner agrees to accept, the sum or sums set forth in subdivision ———— of the annexed Schedule "A," subject to the following conditions:

(a) The term "subsidiary rights" as used in subdivision ———— of the annexed Schedule "A" and elsewhere in this agreement is defined to mean motion picture, radio, television, second-class touring, stock, amateur, foreign language, condensed and tabloid version, foreign (outside of the United States, Canada and the British Isles), commercial tie-in and grand opera rights of the Play.

(b) Any sums payable hereunder to the Owner with respect to first-class legitimate stage productions of the Play in the United States, Canada and the British Isles shall be payable when royalties with respect thereto are paid to the Dramatists and shall be accompanied by customary box office statements. All payments hereunder shall be waived with respect to benefit performances in the United States for the Actors' Fund of America if the Dramatists similarly waive royalties.

(c) Any sums to be paid to the Owner with respect to the disposition of subsidiary rights shall be deemed due and payable as, if and when the net proceeds therefrom are actually received and realized by the Dramatists in cash funds, and the Owner's share thereof shall be computed after the deduction of the share, if any, which any Producer or Manager shall be entitled to receive pursuant to any production contract or contracts for any first-class presentation of the Play and after deduction of customary agents' commissions, Motion Picture Negotiator's fees and reasonable expenses. If the Play be a musical play, the Owner shall not be entitled to share in any proceeds derived from the publication, mechanical reproduction, synchronization and small performing rights in the music and lyrics of the Play or proceeds derived from ASCAP, BMI or similar societies throughout the world, or from any use of the separate musical compositions of the Play for motion picture, radio, television or any other purpose.

(d) All payments to the Owner hereunder shall be subject to applicable currency exchange control, taxation and other laws, regulations and orders. If any sums in which the Owner shares shall be "blocked," "frozen," or otherwise held in a foreign country, the Owner's share may be deposited upon notice to the Owner in the Owner's name in a bank or other depositary in the foreign country at Owner's risk and subject to applicable foreign law, and such deposit shall be deemed payment to the Owner. The Owner's share of any funds converted from a foreign currency shall be computed at the actual conversion rate used for such conversion.

(e) All sums paid to the Owner on the signing hereof and prior to the first public performance of the Play (whether paid for an extension of the production date or otherwise) shall be deemed nonreturnable advances against the sums payable to the Owner with respect to first-class legitimate stage productions of the Play in the United States, Canada and the British Isles and with respect to the disposition of subsidiary rights of the Play.

FOURTH: In the event the Play shall not be produced and presented on the first-class legitimate stage in the United States on or before the production date set forth in subdivision ———— of Schedule "A" as the same may be extended as provided therein, all rights herein granted to Purchaser shall terminate and revert to the Owner and thereupon the Owner and Purchaser shall be released and discharged from any further liability or obligation to the other except as otherwise expressly provided in this paragraph FOURTH. Upon such termination, neither the Owner nor the Purchaser shall have any right, title or interest in the aforesaid Play or any right to use or authorize the use thereof, except however that any and all music, lyrics (whether or not taken from or suggested by the Work) and musical compositions written and composed for the Play (if it be a musical play) and any and all situations, characters, incidents, plots, dialogue, titles, names and other material originally conceived and created by the Dramatists for the Play (whether or not it be a musical play) and not contained in the Work shall remain the sole and absolute property of the Purchaser and the Dramatists (as their respective interests may appear) with the free and unrestricted right to make any use or disposition thereof as they may desire free from any claim by the Owner for any reason whatsoever.

FIFTH: If the Play shall be produced and presented within the time and in the manner set forth in paragraph FOURTH, then the Work and all rights of every kind and nature therein now or hereafter known and in the copyright and renewal copyright thereof shall be deemed merged in the Play as part thereof, to the same extent as though the Play and the Work were one single work, and the Purchaser shall have, and the Owner does hereby convey, grant and assign to the Purchaser absolutely and forever, the same rights in the Work as are acquired by or vested in the Purchaser hereunder in the Play, together with the right to make and enter into any and all contracts and to exercise all rights and privileges, or to refrain from so doing, with respect thereto as the Purchaser may determine in Purchaser's sole discretion, without the necessity of obtaining the consent, approval, signature or other action by the Owner, provided, however, that if the Work has heretofore been published as set forth in subdivision ———— of Schedule "A," the Owner reserves all book, novel, serial, magazine and newspaper publication rights in and to the present text of the Work and the revenue therefrom, but this reservation shall not restrict or affect the exclusive right of the Purchaser to publish the Play or to use or authorize the use (in connection with the exploitation of motion pictures based on the Play) of synopses, digests or versions of the Work not exceeding 7,500 words in length. It is agreed that the Dramatists of the Play shall be deemed the sole authors of the Play for all purposes (and the Owner shall not be deemed an author or owner thereof for any purposes notwithstanding any other agreement now or hereafter made) and the obligations to the Owner under this agreement shall in no way affect, lessen or impair the rights herein conveyed to the Purchaser, and in the event of any default in the payment of any sum of money or other default under this agreement, the Owner shall not have any right of reversion, rescission, approval or consent, nor can the Owner interfere with any of the rights herein granted, but nothing herein contained shall be construed to restrict the Owner's right under this agreement to actions or proceedings for the recovery of sums payable to the Owner hereunder.

SIXTH: In the event of a merger of rights, as provided in FIFTH hereof, the play and any and all rights therein of every kind and nature, now known or hereafter ascertained, together with all copyrights and renewal or extended copyrights thereof, and all rights appertaining thereto, shall become and remain forever throughout the world the sole, complete, exclusive and absolute property of the Purchaser and Dramatists as their respective interests may appear and as they may elect and agree among themselves.

SEVENTH: All agreements made by the Purchaser relating to the production and presentation of the Play shall provide that in all programs, houseboards and paid advertising (other than daily ABC ads), the Author's name shall appear whenever the Dramatists' names appear, substantially in the form set forth in subdivision ———— of Schedule "A."

EIGHTH: Commencing on the date hereof and until the termination of the rights granted to the Purchaser, and of the rights which may become vested in the Dramatists and their heirs, next-of-kin, representatives, successors and assigns, and any owner of any copyrights of the said Play, the Owner agrees not to grant, sell, assign, encumber or otherwise dispose of, or exercise or permit others to exercise, any rights of whatsoever kind or nature in the Work or any part thereof or in any versions, adaptations and/or sequels thereof or perform or do any act with respect thereto which may in any way diminish, invalidate, impair, affect or interfere with the full exercise and enjoyment of the rights granted hereunder, except only for the publication rights expressly reserved in paragraph FIFTH hereof.

NINTH: The Owner agrees prior to the expiration of any copyright or copyrights in the Work, as the same may be extended, to renew or extend or procure the renewal or extension of any such copyright or copyrights and grant and assign to the Purchaser for such renewal or extended terms all the same rights herein granted and assigned to the Purchaser for the original copyright term. The Owner hereby irrevocably appoints the Purchaser and each of the Dramatists as the Owner's attorney-in-fact to execute, deliver and record, on behalf of the Owner and in the name of the Owner or otherwise, any and all documents necessary or proper to secure the renewal or extension of any such copyright or copyrights and all rights therein for the term of such renewal or extension, and to execute, deliver and record, on behalf of the Owner and in the Owner's name or otherwise, any and all assignments and other documents necessary or proper to convey, grant and assign to the Purchaser the rights hereby conveyed, granted and assigned, for the term of such renewal or extension. The Owner agrees that, in the event that the present Copyright Law of the United States of America, or any other country where said Work is or may hereafter be protected by copyright, shall be amended or changed or a new Copyright Law enacted, so that the term of the copyright is extended or enlarged, the Purchaser shall forthwith and automatically become entitled for such enlarged or extended term to all the rights hereby conveyed, granted and assigned to the Purchaser for the present term of copyright and renewal copyright, or the equivalent thereof to the maximum extent permitted by but subject to such new Copyright Law.

The Purchaser shall require the Dramatists of the Play to duly copyright the Play and take all steps and acts necessary to secure such copyright all to the end that the Work shall not fall into the public domain.

TENTH: To the extent the Owner reserves publication rights hereunder, the Owner agrees not to publish or permit the publication of the Work in any country of the world unless the same shall be duly copyrighted and all steps and acts taken to secure such copyright, all to the end that the Work shall not fall into the public domain.

ELEVENTH: The parties hereto agree to do and perform any acts and execute any and all documents that may be necessary to carry out and effectuate the purpose and intent of this agreement. If the Owner shall fail to execute and deliver any such documents, the Purchaser and the Dramatists are each hereby irrevocably empowered and authorized to execute and deliver any such documents in the Owner's name as Owner's attorney-in-fact.

TWELFTH: The Owner hereby agrees to defend, indemnify and hold harmless the Purchaser and the Dramatists and others claiming by, through or under them from and against any and all claims, liability, losses, damages, judgments, costs and expenses, including reasonable counsel fees, which may be made against or suffered or incurred by the Purchaser and/or the Dramatists and such others growing out of or by reason of any claims made with respect to, or any breach or non-performance of, any warranty, representation, agreement or undertaking of the Owner hereunder, it being understood that the foregoing shall not apply to any material added by the Dramatists which is not contained in the Work.

THIRTEENTH: In the event of any dispute between the parties hereto (or their respective successors and assigns) arising under, out of, or in connection with the within agreement or the Play, or the breach of this agreement, its performance, interpretation, validity or making, the same shall be determined by arbitration in New York City, pursuant to the rules of the American Arbitration Association in force at the time, and any award rendered as a result thereof shall be final and conclusive upon the parties, and judgment thereon may be entered in the highest of the forum (State, Federal or otherwise) having jurisdiction; provided that such arbitration shall be held before three (3) arbitrators, one to be selected by the claimant or claimants, one by the respondent or respondents and one from the panel of the Association by the arbitrators so selected. The arbitrators are empowered in addition to all other powers conferred by law or the said rules to award specific performance and temporary or permanent injunctions (including mandatory injunctions) and restraints, partial relief, damages, costs and expenses and pre-hearing or post-hearing discovery, inspection, depositions and accountings and to make any awards which may be just and fair to effectuate the purposes hereunder.

FOURTEENTH: The Purchaser shall have the right to produce the Play as producer alone or in association with another party or parties, or to arrange for the production solely by another party or parties. The Owner shall not be entitled to any share of moneys received by the Purchaser or any of the Dramatists in their capacity as producers or associate producers of the Play. Nothing herein contained shall prevent the Purchaser and/or the Dramatists from rendering additional services in connection with the production of the Play or the exercise of any rights therein or from receiving compensation therefor, all of which shall at all times be their sole and exclusive property and the Owner shall not be entitled to any share or percentage thereof.

FIFTEENTH: All sums of money payable to the Owner hereunder shall be paid to the order of and sent to the address first above written. All payments shall be accompanied by appropriate and customary statements, and the Owner shall have access at all reasonable times for inspection of relevant books and records of the Purchaser with respect to dispositions of rights in the Play in the proceeds of which the Owner shares.

SIXTEENTH: This agreement shall not constitute the parties hereto as partners or create a joint venture or fiduciary relationship between them, and neither the Owner nor the Purchaser shall be deemed to be the representative or agent of each other except as herein expressly provided. This agreement, together with any and all Schedules hereto attached, constitutes the entire understanding between the parties with respect to the subject matter hereof, and no party has made any representation, warranty or agreement, express or implied, not herein expressly set forth. All matters concerning this agreement and its validity, performance or breach shall be governed by the laws of the State of New York. This agreement shall be binding upon and endure to the benefit of the parties and their respective heirs, executors, administrators, successors and assigns. No agreement changing, amending, extending, superseding, rescinding, terminating, or discharging this agreement or any provisions hereof shall be valid unless in writing and signed by the party to be charged. No waiver of any provisions hereunder shall be binding unless in writing and signed by the party to be charged; no waiver of any breach hereof shall be construed to be a continuing waiver or consent to any subsequent breach hereof.

SEVENTEENTH: Wherever the term "Owner" or "Purchaser" is used and there shall be more than one Owner and/or more than one Purchaser, as evidenced from their signatures below, "Owner" shall mean "Owners" and "Purchaser" shall mean "Purchasers," as the case may be, and their obligations and liabilities hereunder shall be joint and several.

IN WITNESS WHEREOF, the parties hereto have executed this agreement the day and year first above written.

_____
Owner

_____
Purchaser

Form III

AGREEMENT made this ———— day of ————————, 19——,
by and between ——————————————, hereinafter referred
to as "Owner," and ————————————————, hereinafter referred to as "Purchaser."

WITNESSETH

In consideration of the respective covenants herein contained
the parties hereto agree as follows:

1. Owner is the sole author and proprietor without encumbrance
of all motion picture and allied rights in certain literary, musical
and/or dramatic material entitled ———————————————— and
in the extricable component elements thereof including without
limitation characters, character names, plots, dialogue, title, and all
other elements susceptible of repetition in serial form in any medium
such as a television spin-off series, all of which are hereinafter collectively referred to as the "Property."

2. Owner hereby warrants and represents as follows:

(a) He is the sole author of the Property, first published by
———————————————— under the title ———————————————— on
———————————— 19——, and duly registered for copyright in the United
States of America by and in the name of ————————————————
under the title ———————————————— on ———————————— 19——,
Entry No. ————.

(b) The Property is wholly original with Owner in all respects
and no part thereof is, or was taken from, or based upon, any other
literary, dramatic or musical work or any motion picture or writing
not in the public domain.

(c) The Property and any and all parts thereof do not infringe
in any way upon and in no way invade or violate the common law,
or the literary, dramatic or motion picture rights, or the right of
privacy, or any other civil or property rights or other right of any
party whomsoever.

(d) He is the sole Owner of all the rights, licenses, privileges
and property hereunder granted to Purchaser and has full right and
authority to convey the rights herein granted. So far as he knows, no
motion picture has been produced which is, or has been, based on the
Property, in whole or in part. No right, license or privilege to produce

a motion picture derived from the Property has been heretofore granted to any person, firm or corporation and the motion picture rights to the Property, or any part thereof, have in no way been sold, mortgaged, or otherwise disposed of, and are free and clear of any liens whatsoever in favor of any party whomsoever. Owner has done no act or thing by grant or otherwise, and there are no outstanding contracts, rights, privileges, licenses, property or grants of any nature or kind, which will impair the rights, licenses, privileges and property in and to the Property herein granted to Purchaser that will or may prevent in any manner or interfere with the full enjoyment of such rights, licenses, privileges or property by Purchaser, its assignees and licensees. There are no claims or litigation pending or threatened adversely affecting the Property or the copyrights therein or titles thereof or the said rights, licenses and privileges herein conveyed.

(e) Owner has entered into an agreement with _____ _____. Owner agrees that any and all further publication agreements hereafter made by Owner, his agents, licensees or assigns, will contain a provision conditioning the license and authority to publish upon the requirement that there shall be affixed to each copy of the Property or of any volume in which it may be included and which is published or offered for sale, such notice as may be necessary for copyright protection in the United States and under the Universal Copyright Convention, and (if reasonably possible) a further provision that copies of the Property shall be simultaneously published or offered for sale in the Dominion of Canada, in England, or in some country which is a signatory of the International Copyright Convention, sometimes known as the "Berne Convention." The last requirement of the foregoing sentence shall be deemed complied with if reasonable efforts are made to insure that a provision is inserted in any such contract requiring at least ten (10) copies to be publicly offered for sale or public distribution in such country on the same day and date as in the United States. Owner undertakes and agrees to take all reasonable steps, other than legal proceedings, necessary to enforce said provisions, and in the event of a breach thereof, will assign to Purchaser, to the extent Purchaser has been damaged thereby, all of the proceeds and benefits of any suit or proceeding instituted or undertaken at the request of and at the expense of Purchaser for the enforcement of such provision in accordance therewith. Owner warrants that he has made no grant to any party of any rights in the Property (exclusive or non-exclusive in nature) which could or may in any wise interfere with the full-time use of the rights acquired by Purchaser hereunder.

Owner further agrees specifically to except and reserve the rights or interest in and to the Property, which are herein granted, when any grant is made by Owner to others of any other rights or interests. Owner shall not be deemed to have granted hereafter any rights inconsistent with those granted to Purchaser hereunder if each contract made by Owner or any successor in interest making any grant of rights in connection with the Property shall contain a provision without diminishing the scope of the grant of rights hereunder reading substantially in the following form: "Any rights herein granted are subject and subordinate to all rights of every kind and nature granted to or acquired by (name of purchaser) pursuant to its agreement with (name of owner) dated _____, relating to that certain property entitled (name of work)." The fact that Purchaser shall, without the written consent of Owner, have made any settlement with any third party making claims which, if sustained, would constitute a breach of a representation, warranty or covenant hereunder, shall not be determinative of the liability, if any, of Owner to Purchaser.

3. Owner hereby irrevocably grants, sells, assigns, transfers and sets over to Purchaser, exclusively and forever, all and entire motion picture rights of any kind and nature whatsoever, in and to the Property (including each and every part thereof) and in and to any incident, characters, character names, scenes, sequences or characterizations therein contained including (but not in limitation thereof) the entire silent, sound, dialogue and talking and musical motion picture rights and the televised motion picture rights therein and in all languages for the entire world, such rights being hereinafter included in and embraced in the expression "motion picture rights," including the story line, plot, development and title of the Property together with all of the benefits of the copyrights and common law rights and the right to secure copyright in and to the motion pictures in the United States of America and all other countries of the world where copyright is obtainable, at the expense of and in the name of Purchaser or otherwise, and of all remedies for enforcing such copyrights with respect to the motion picture rights and all other rights herein granted to Purchaser.

Included among the rights conveyed, but not in limitation thereof, are the rights hereinafter set forth:

(a) The exclusive right at any time or times to make one or more motion picture versions or adaptations of the Property or of any part thereof, and to produce, issue, reproduce, remake, or reissue one or more motion picture versions and sequel motion picture versions based thereon of any type now known, or hereafter to be known, including negative and positive prints thereof, of any size or type (all of which are hereinafter sometimes referred to collectively as the "motion picture") and the exclusive right to show or project or broadcast or exhibit same in any manner and on any surface known, or to be known; however, Purchaser shall not have the right to serialize any motion picture made hereunder but shall have the right to show same in installments limited to mean exhibition on television broken by commercial inserts and/or in not more than two-part showings and in theatres broken by intermissions.

(b) The exclusive right to record and reproduce language, speech, dialogue, music and any other sound (including foreign language) in synchronism with the production, exhibition and distribution of said photoplay and/or motion picture based upon the Property or Purchaser's adaptations thereof, whether such recordings be on the film itself, or on separate disks, or otherwise, by means of any devices known or to be known, and which are now used, or hereafter may be used, invented or discovered, in connection with the production, exhibition or distribution of the motion picture. All films or disks or other material on which sounds are now recorded, or hereafter may be recorded for use in connection with and/or in synchronism with the motion picture, are hereinafter referred to as "sound records."

(c) The exclusive right to distribute, sell, lease, exhibit, license for exhibition and in any other manner exploit and dispose of throughout the world for public and/or private performances, said photoplay and/or motion picture versions based upon the Property and all sound records produced and used in connection therewith.

(d) The exclusive right to secure copyright registration (or, in the countries where no copyright law exists, equivalent protection) of motion picture versions and of such sound records in connection therewith in all countries of the world under the then existing laws of such countries in the name of Purchaser or any other person, firm or corporation.

(e) The exclusive right for the purpose of making motion pictures and, for the purpose of exploiting the same, to make any and all changes, translations, additions, deletions and substitutions to and from the Property or its title, or titles, which Purchaser may desire, and to adapt, rearrange, add to or take from its literary and dramatic materials, and to use lines, excerpts and adaptations therefrom in titles, text, sound records and otherwise in connection with the making or exhibition of the motion picture and/or sound records produced in connection therewith.

(f) The exclusive right in connection with the motion picture to interpolate music, lyrics, sound, noises, songs, words, language, dialogue or titles in the Property or to make any other adaptations, arrangements, dramatizations, changes, transpositions, translations or interpolations thereof or in addition thereto or deletions therefrom which Purchaser may desire for the exclusive purposes of, and in connection with, the producing, reproducing, distributing, exploiting and/or exhibiting such photoplay or motion picture and/or sound records, and to record the same on sound records produced in connection therewith, and to produce the same from such sound records.

(g) The exclusive right to project by television, electronically, or in any manner now known, or hereafter devised, for the simultaneous transmission of sight and sound, including magnetic tape and magnetic wire, any motion picture based on the Property, including sound, talking, singing and other audible portions thereof through space, or by cable where toll charges are imposed on the viewer, for exhibition and performance at any and all places in and/or away from that wherein such motion picture version shall be exhibited and performed; provided, however, that no motion picture (including any remake, sequel or musical motion picture) shall be broadcast serially.

(h) In addition, Purchaser shall have the following radio and television rights in connection with the exhibition of each motion picture produced hereunder, to wit: The right to broadcast by radio and television, using live actors, or otherwise, dramatic versions and sketches based upon and adapted from such motion picture version based upon and adapted from the Property. Such broadcasts shall not exceed ten (10) minutes per program, and there shall be no right to serialize said radio and television versions; provided, however, that Owner will negotiate in good faith respecting additional time that might enhance the value of the Property, e.g., on the "Ed Sullivan Show," and similarly respecting the possibility that two such radio broadcasts may be for periods not to exceed thirty (30) minutes in any country wherein the motion picture version may be released, both in connection with its first general release and with any subsequent reissue thereof. In addition, Purchaser shall have the right to broadcast by television, or any other electronic or other device now known or hereafter devised or known for the simultaneous or substantially simultaneous transmission of sound and sight, including magnetic tape and magnetic wire, scenes from the negative and sound track of the motion picture version not to exceed fifteen (15) minutes in length. Nothing herein contained shall be deemed to limit Purchaser's right in connection with such limited television showings of the film to use live actors for interview purposes in connection with any motion picture hereunder, not hereinabove in this paragraph restricted. The Owner agrees (without otherwise limiting his reserved rights in the original Property hereunder, viz., stage rights and other rights not granted) to withhold the exercise of the reserved television rights until seven (7) years from the first release of the first motion picture produced hereunder, or ten (10) years from the date of this Agreement, whichever shall be later and to withhold the exercise of the reserved radio rights for a similar time.

The live television rights herein reserved to the Owner do not include (i) the right to film or reproduce any live television broadcast by kinescope process, or by magnetic tape, magnetic wire, or by any other contrivance, device or method, whether similar or dissimilar or whether now known or hereafter known, invented or devised, except for one use within sixty (60) days from the date of each live broadcast in any television market (as such term is understood in the television industry) in the United States and Canada and in any areas of any country or territory which did not carry such live broadcast, provided further that, if instead of making direct broadcast of a live television performance, such live performance is recorded on tape or other similar process and such recording (entirely without interruption, editing or alteration of any kind) is initially broadcast within ten days after such recording, such recording, hereinafter called the "tape," shall, for the purpose of this paragraph only, be treated as having been made as a live broadcast, and such one further use may be made of such tape during said 60-day period, in the same manner as in respect of a live broadcast; (ii) the right to exercise same for transmission and projection through space for exhibition or reproduction at any theatre and/or similar place of public assembly at which an admission fee is charged to see such telecast away from that wherein the same shall be projected or performed by television, electronically or in any other manner or by any other method, whether now known or hereafter known, invented or devised; and (iii) the right to exhibit or reproduce a performance of any kind by means of subscription television, whether the audience pays directly or indirectly or whether the payment be made by means of cash, tokens or credit, or in any other manner or by any other method whether now known or hereafter known, invented or devised, until seven years from the first release of the first motion picture produced hereunder or ten years from the date of the Option agreement, whichever shall be later and subject to the provisions of the following paragraph.

In the event that the Owner, at such time as he may exercise his reserved live television rights, determines to dispose of same, or any interest therein, he will give the Purchaser the first right and opportunity to acquire same on the same terms and conditions of any bona fide offer that the Owner may determine to accept, there being however no obligation upon the Owner to dispose of such television rights or interest therein at any time or for any price, unless he elects so to do. When, as and if the Owner shall receive a bona fide offer for the reserved television rights and interest therein, which he is willing to accept, he shall send the Purchaser written notice thereof which notice shall comprehend all of the terms of such offer. Upon receipt thereof, the Purchaser shall, within five (5) days, exclusive of Saturdays, Sundays and holidays, thereafter, either accept or reject such offer. Should it accept the terms of said offer, then the Owner shall grant to the Purchaser such television rights or interest so offered on the same terms and conditions as are set forth in the aforesaid offer. Should the Purchaser reject or fail to accept such offer within five (5) days, exclusive of Saturdays, Sundays and holidays, then Owner shall be free to dispose of such television rights and interest therein upon the terms offered to the Purchaser, but Owner shall not sell or dispose of such rights upon any other terms without first again offering such rights to Purchaser upon such other terms. If at any time Purchaser shall accept any such offer made by Owner of such television rights or interest therein, the Owner agrees not to grant or offer to grant in any country referred to in said offer any television rights (not previously acquired by Purchaser) for a period of six (6) months from and after said acceptance by Purchaser.

(i) The exclusive right to advertise and exploit motion pictures based upon the Property and, for purposes of advertising and exploiting such motion pictures, but not otherwise, to publish, provided then existing copyright or right of copyright in the United States shall not thereby be impaired, excerpts, summaries, synopses and stories of the Property and the motion pictures based upon the Property in heralds, booklets, programs, posters, lobby displays, press books and newspapers, magazines and other periodicals, and to copyright the same in the name of the Purchaser, and to produce and distribute trailers and other forms of short motion pictures, accompanied or unaccompanied by sound records, synchronized therewith for exhibition in theatres in advance of the exhibition of such motion pictures. Such excerpts, summaries, synopses and stories of the Property shall not exceed 10,000 words in each such instance and shall not be serialized, and no such excerpts, summary, synopsis or story shall appear as having been written by Owner. Such excerpts, summaries, synopses and stories may also be used and sold as part of so-called program books, but no right is otherwise hereby granted separately to publish or sell any such excerpts, summaries, synopses or stories in book form irrespective of whether same be hard or soft cover.

(j) The exclusive right to use for motion pictures made hereunder based in whole or in part upon the Property, the title(s) by which the Property is now known.

(k) The exclusive right to use for motion pictures in all of the ways hereinabove set forth any and all dramatic and musical material including without limitation book, music and lyrics interpolated in connection with any dramatic or dramatico-musical production of the Property in any medium in accordance with any rights reserved by the Owner hereunder. The Owner agrees that he will not exercise such reserved rights or make any commitments therefor without a symmetrical agreement from the authors of the book, music and lyrics in favor of Purchaser hereunder together with any consents or waivers required by any Guild or Union having jurisdiction.

(1) Any additional rights reasonably required by a major financier-distributor of feature motion pictures with whom Purchaser shall have made arrangements for the distribution of a motion picture based on the Property hereunder. Nothing in this agreement or in the Option Agreement of even date herewith shall be interpreted or construed to obligate Purchaser to produce any motion picture or other version of the Property or to exercise any of the other rights, licenses or privileges herein conveyed or to complete any of the acts recited in this clause once undertaken.

4. Owner will indemnify and hold harmless the Purchaser, its agents, licensees, successors and assigns from any and all damages, costs, recoveries, judgments, penalties and reasonable counsel fees that may be obtained against, imposed upon or suffered by Purchaser, its agents, licensees, successors and assigns by reason of the breach of any of the representations, warranties or covenants of said Owner herein contained.

5. Without in any wise limiting the generality of the grants hereinabove made, Owner acknowledges that Purchaser is now acquiring, among other rights, the right to produce musical motion picture versions and sequel versions to any motion picture version or remake of the work, which it may produce hereunder, and that such rights, subject only to reversion for Purchaser's default hereunder, are hereby vested in the Purchaser irrevocably.

Purchaser agrees that if after the production of the first motion picture version hereunder, it shall produce a sequel motion picture version of its own, or a remake of such motion picture, then upon the commencement of principal photography of such sequel or remake motion picture, Purchaser shall pay to Owner for the right to make such sequel or remake, an additional sum in the amount of $————. The term "sequel" as used herein in this Article shall be deemed to signify a motion picture:

(a) That is produced after there shall have been produced the first motion picture (or a remake or remakes thereof) pursuant to the grants herein made by Owner;

(b) In which the leading character or characters is or are taken from the work or one of the said motion pictures referred to in (a) hereof or a sequel thereof;

(c) In which the characters are shown as participating for the most part in new and different events than those in which such characters participated in the work or any motion picture referred to in (a) hereof, or in any preceding "sequel"; and

(d) In which the story of such subsequent motion picture is substantially different than as set forth in (a) the Property or (b) any such preceding picture.

6. The Owner will, if requested in writing so to do, during the period when copyright renewal may be applied for, or at any time within six (6) months prior thereto, secure or cause to be secured renewals of the copyrights procured by the Owner in the United States of America of the Property and of any translations, revisions and reissues thereof owned by Owner, at least six months prior to the expiration of the original copyrights therein, and Owner will duly execute or cause to be executed any and all instruments necessary to vest rights herein granted in Purchaser and to execute any and all further documents and instruments necessary to effectuate the intention of the parties hereto. In the event of the failure of Owner to do any and all of the acts necessary to obtain such renewals within the time hereinabove specified, or to effectuate such extension, Owner hereby appoints Purchaser his irrevocable attorney-in-fact with the right (but Purchaser shall not be obligated) to execute and file all such documents and to do any and all acts and things necessary for the obtaining of such renewal or such extension for the benefit of Purchaser, without prejudice to any and all rights of Purchaser to require Owner to obtain the copyright renewal to and vest the rights herein granted to Purchaser. The obligation of Owner to execute instruments as in this paragraph provided shall only exist to the extent that Owner can legally agree so to do.

7. During the terms of the rights granted to the Purchaser hereunder, Owner will and does hereby appoint Purchaser his irrevocable attorney-in-fact with the right (but Purchaser shall not be obligated to) and at the sole expense of and for the sole benefit of Purchaser, to enforce and protect all motion picture rights, licenses, privileges or property herein granted under any and all copyrights thereof in and to the Property, to prevent any infringement of said copyright (but only if the rights herein granted to the Purchaser are thereby affected) and to litigate, collect and receipt for all damages arising from such infringement of said rights, licenses and privileges, property and/or copyrights (to the extent Purchaser has been damaged) in and to the work conveyed to Purchaser, using the name of Owner, in the discretion of the Purchaser.

8. In consideration of all of the grants herein made and all of the rights herein granted, sold and assigned, Purchaser agrees to pay to Owner an aggregate consideration in the amount of $———— of which amount the sum of $———— has already been paid simultaneously with execution of the Option Agreement of even date herewith, leaving a balance of $———— payable upon condition that the option therein provided for is exercised and the instant Property Agreement thereby made effective.

All sums of money due under this agreement shall be paid to the Owner's agent, ———————————— and the receipt of the said ———————————— shall be a good and valid dis-

charge of all such indebtedness; and the said _____
is hereby empowered by the Owner to act in all matters arising
from this agreement. The Owner does hereby assign and transfer to
_____ and _____ shall retain
the sum equal to ten per cent (10%), as an agency coupled with
an interest, out of all monies due and payable to and for the account
of the Owner under this agreement.

9. With respect to the foregoing payments, Purchaser shall not
be deemed in default if payment of any amount hereunder shall
ultimately or by temporary court order be enjoined, restrained or
prevented by judicial process or if at or prior to the time that
any payment shall be due hereunder an action or proceeding shall
have been instituted against Purchaser in which a judgment for the
plaintiff therein would constitute a breach of the warranties and representation herein made by Owner, all however subject to payment
to Owner hereunder if such action or proceeding is ultimately dis-
missed. Notice of the institution of any such action shall be given to
Owner and an opportunity to join in the defense thereof at no expense
to Purchaser.

10. Purchaser agrees, with respect to the motion picture versions that it may make hereunder, to cause the same to be registered
for copyright in the United States in the name of Purchaser as copyright owner if Purchaser so elects, and to cause to be affixed on the
negative of such motion picture versions exhibited to the public, a
notice that the motion picture has been copyrighted in the United
States, and the year of such copyright, provided, however, that no
failure to comply with the terms of this sentence shall impose any
liability on Purchaser if such failure has been occasioned or caused
under such circumstances as not to affect or impair the validity of
the Copyright Owner's reserved rights in and to the aforesaid Property. In addition:

(a) Subject to error, inadvertent omission and circumstances
beyond Purchaser's control the Owner will be given billing credit in
connection with any motion picture hereunder as author of the
underlying Property. Such billing credit will be as provided hereinafter in sub-paragraph (b).

(b)

11. Owner will execute, acknowledge and deliver, or cause to be executed, acknowledged and delivered to Purchaser, any and all further assignments or other instruments which may be necessary or expedient to carry out and effectuate the purposes and intent of this agreement.

12. Wherever in this agreement reference is made to the Owner, it shall be deemed to embrace and include the Owner's heirs, executors, administrators, next of kin, successors and assigns, and whatever reference has been made to the Purchaser, such reference shall be deemed to include and embrace its successors and assigns, and Purchaser shall have the free, full, unrestricted and unlimited right to sell, assign, transfer or otherwise dispose of this agreement and/or any or all of its right, title and interest thereunder, in whole or in part, provided that any such assignee or transferee shall assume all of Purchaser's obligations hereunder.

13. This agreement shall be binding upon and inure to the benefit of Owner, his heirs, administrators and assigns, and shall be binding upon and inure to the benefit of Purchaser, its successors and assigns.

14. All notices and communications required under the terms of this agreement to be delivered shall be deemed delivered when deposited, postage prepaid, registered from any post office box or post office in the United States, addressed as follows:

Owner:
Purchaser:

15. This agreement is to be construed and is to take effect as a contract made and performed or to be performed under the laws of the State of New York and shall be governed in all respects by the laws of the State of New York.

IN WITNESS WHEREOF, the parties hereto have hereunto set their hands and seals the day and year first hereinabove written.

_____
Owner

_____
Purchaser

Form IV

AGREEMENT made this ———— day of ————————————,
19——, between RANDOM HOUSE, INC., of 457 Madison Avenue,
New York, N.Y. 10022 (referred to as the Publisher), and

whose address is

who is a citizen of ———————————— and resident of (state)
———————————— (referred to as the Author and designated
by the masculine singular pronoun)

WHEREAS the parties wish respectively to publish and have
published a work (referred to as the work) of ————————
———————— provisionally titled

NOW, THEREFORE, they mutually agree as follows:

Grant of Rights
1. The Author grants to the Publisher during the term of copyright, including renewals and extensions thereof:

a. Exclusive right in the English language, in the United States of America, the Philippine Republic, and Canada, and non-exclusive right in all other countries except the British Commonwealth (other than Canada), the Republic of South Africa, and the Irish Republic, to:

i. Print, publish and sell the work in book form;

ii. License publication of the work (in complete, condensed or abridged versions) by book clubs, including subsidiaries of the Publisher;

iii. License publication of a reprint edition by another publisher with the consent of the Author. The Author shall be deemed to have given consent if within twenty (20) days after the forwarding of written request he fails to notify the Publisher in writing of his refusal to consent;

iv. License publication of the work (in complete, condensed, adapted or abridged versions) or selections from the work in anthologies and other publications, in mail-order and schoolbook editions, as premiums and other special editions and through microfilm and with the Author's consent Xerox or other forms of copying;

v. License periodical publication including magazines, newspapers and digests prior to book publication;

vi. License periodical publication after book publication to the extent that any such right is available;

vii. License, subject to the approval of the Author, adaptation of the work for filmstrips, printed cartoon versions and mechanical reproduction;

viii. License, without charge, transcription or publication of the work in Braille or in other forms, for the physically handicapped;

ix. For publicity purposes, publish or permit others to publish or broadcast (but not dramatize) by radio or television, without charge, such selections from the work as in the opinion of the Publisher may benefit its sale.

b. Exclusive right to license in the English language throughout the British Commonwealth (other than Canada), the Republic of South Africa, and the Irish Republic, the rights granted in subdivision a. above, revocable by the Author with respect to any country for which no license or option has been given within eighteen (18) months after first publication in the United States.

c. Exclusive right to license in all foreign languages and all countries, the rights granted in subdivision a. above, revocable by the Author with respect to each language or country for which no license or option has been given within three (3) years after first publication in the United States.

d. Exclusive right to use or license others to use, subject to the approval of the Author, the name and likeness of the Author, the work and the title of the work, in whole or in part, or any adaptation thereof as the basis for trademark or trade name for other products or for any other commercial use in connection with such other products.

Delivery of Satisfactory Copy

2. The Author agrees to deliver two complete copies (original and clean copy) of the manuscript of the work in the English language of approximately ———— words in length, in content and form satisfactory to the Publisher, together with any permission required pursuant to Paragraph 3, and all photographs, illustrations, drawings, charts, maps and indexes suitable for reproduction and necessary to the completion of the manuscript not later than ————————————————. If he fails to do so the Publisher shall have the right to supply them and charge the cost against any sums accruing to the Author. The complete manuscript shall include the following additional items:

If the Author fails to deliver the manuscript within ninety (90) days after the above date the Publisher may terminate this agreement by giving written notice, whereupon the Author agrees to repay forthwith all amounts which may have been advanced hereunder.

Permission for Copyrighted Material

3. If the Author incorporates in the work any copyrighted material, he shall procure, at his expense, written permission to reprint it.

Author's Warranties and Indemnities

4. a. The Author warrants that he is the sole author of the work; that he is the sole owner of all the rights granted to the Publisher; that he has not previously assigned, pledged or otherwise encumbered the same; that he has full power to enter into this agreement; that except for the material obtained pursuant to Paragraph 3 the work is original, has not been published before, and is not in the public domain; that it does not violate any right of privacy; that it is not libelous or obscene; that it does not infringe upon any statutory or common law copyright; and that any recipe, formula or instruction contained in the work is not injurious to the user.

b. In the event of any claim, action or proceeding based upon an alleged violation of any of these warranties (i) the Publisher shall have the right to defend the same through counsel of its own choosing, and (ii) no settlement shall be effected without the prior written consent of the Author, which consent shall not unreasonably be withheld, and (iii) the Author shall hold harmless the Publisher, any seller of the work, and any licensee of a subsidiary right in the work, against any damages finally sustained. If such claim, action or proceeding is successfully defended or settled, the Author's indemnity hereunder shall be limited to fifty per cent (50%) of the expense (including reasonable counsel fees) attributable to such defense or settlement; however, such limitation of liability shall not apply if the claim, action or proceeding is based on copyright infringement.

c. If any such claim, action or proceeding is instituted, the Publisher shall promptly notify the Author, who shall fully cooperate in the defense thereof, and the Publisher may withhold payments of reasonable amounts due him under this or any other agreement between the parties.

d. These warranties and indemnities shall survive the termination of this agreement.

Conflicting Publication

5. The Author agrees that during the term of this agreement he will not, without the written permission of the Publisher, publish or permit to be published any material, in book or pamphlet form, based on material in the work.

Date, Style and Price of Publication

6. Within one year after the Author has delivered the manuscript in conformity with Paragraph 2, the Publisher shall publish the work at its own expense, in such style and manner, under such imprint and at such price as it deems suitable. The Publisher shall not be responsible for delays caused by any circumstance beyond its control. No changes in the manuscript or the provisional title shall be made without the consent of the Author. However, in no event shall the Publisher be obligated to publish a work which in its opinion violates the common law or statutory copyright or the right of privacy of any person or contains libelous or obscene matter.

Proofreading and Author's Corrections

7. The Author agrees to read, revise, correct and return promptly all proofs of the work and to pay in cash or, at the option of the Publisher, to have charged against him, the cost of alterations, in type or in plates, required by the Author, other than those due to printer's errors, in excess of ten per cent (10%) of the cost of setting

type, provided a statement of these charges is sent to the Author within thirty (30) days of the receipt of the printer's bills and the corrected proofs are presented on request for his inspection.

Copyright

8. The Publisher shall copyright the work in the name of the Author, in the United States, in compliance with the Universal Copyright Convention, and apply for renewals of such copyright. If copyright should be in the name of the Publisher, it shall assign such copyright upon request of the Author. The Publisher agrees to arrange for the sale of the work in Canada. If the Publisher adds illustrations or other material, and if copyright is in the Author's name, he agrees, upon request, to assign the copyright of such material. If the Author retains the right to periodical or foreign publication before publication by the Publisher, he shall notify the Publisher promptly of any arrangement of such publication or any postponement thereof. In the event of a periodical publication, if the copyright shall be in the name of any person other than the Author, he shall promptly deliver to the Publisher a legally recordable assignment of such copyright or of the rights granted. In the event of a publication outside the United States, promptly thereafter, he shall furnish to the Publisher three copies of the first published work and the date of such publication.

Advance Payments

9. The Publisher shall pay to the Author as an advance against and on account of all moneys accruing to him under this agreement, the sum of _____ dollars ($_____), payable

Any such advance shall not be repayable, provided that the Author has delivered the manuscript in conformity with Paragraph 2 and is not otherwise in default under this agreement.

Royalty Payments

10. The Publisher shall pay to the Author a royalty on the retail price of every copy sold by the Publisher, less returns (except as set forth below):

    a.   per cent (%) up to and including _____ copies;
          per cent (%) in excess of _____ copies up to and including _____ copies; and _____ per cent (%) in excess of _____ copies.

Where the discount in the United States is forty-eight per cent
(48%) or more from the retail price, the rate provided in this subdivision a. shall be reduced by one-half the difference between forty-
four per cent (44%) and the discount granted. In no event, however,
shall such royalty be less than one-half of the rate provided herein.
If the semi-annual sales aggregate fewer than 400 copies, the royalty
shall be two-thirds (⅔) of the rate provided in this subdivision a. if
such copies are sold from a second or subsequent printing. Copies
covered by any other subdivision of this Paragraph shall not be included in such computation.

Mail Order Sales

b. Five per cent (5%) of the amount received for copies sold
directly to the consumer through the medium of mail-order or coupon
advertising, or radio or television advertising.

Premiums and Subscriptions

c. Five per cent (5%) of the amount received for copies sold by
the Publisher's Premium or Subscription Books Wholesale Department.

College Sales

d. Ten per cent (10%) for hard-cover copies and five per cent
(5%) for soft-cover copies sold with a lower retail price as college
textbooks.

School Editions

e. For a School edition the royalty provided in subdivision a. of
this Paragraph but no more than:
    i. Ten per cent (10%) of the amount received for a Senior
High School edition;
    ii. Eight per cent (8%) of the amount received for a Junior
High School edition;
    iii. Six per cent (6%) of the amount received for an Ele-
mentary School-edition.

Lower-price Editions

f. Five per cent (5%) for an edition published at a lower retail
price or for an edition in the Modern Library (regular or giant size)
or in Vintage Books; and two per cent (2%) or two cents (2¢) per
copy, whichever is greater, for an edition in the Modern Library
College Editions.

Export Sales

g. Ten per cent (10%) of the amount received for the original edition and five per cent (5%) of the amount received for any lower-price edition for copies sold for export.

Special Sales

h. For copies sold outside normal wholesale and retail trade channels, ten per cent (10%) of the amount received for the original edition and five per cent (5%) of the amount received for any lower-price edition for copies sold at a discount between fifty per cent (50%) and sixty per cent (60%) from the retail price and five per cent (5%) of the amount received for copies sold at a discount of sixty per cent (60%) or more from the retail price, or for the use of the plates by any governmental agency.

No Royalty Copies

i. No royalty shall be paid on copies sold below or at cost including expenses incurred, or furnished gratis to the Author, or for review, advertising, sample or like purposes.

Receipts From Other Rights

j. Fifty per cent (50%) of the amount received from the disposition of licenses granted pursuant to Paragraph 1, subdivision a., ii, iii, iv, vi and vii. At the Author's request his share from book club and reprint licensing, less any unearned advances, shall be paid to him within two weeks after the receipt thereof by the Publisher. If the Publisher rebates to booksellers for unsold copies due to the publication of a lower-price or reprint edition, the royalty on such copies shall be the same as for such lower-price edition.

First Serial

k. Ninety per cent (90%) of the amount received from the disposition of licenses in the United States and Canada granted pursuant to Paragraph 1, subdivision a., v.

British

l. Eighty per cent (80%) of the amount received from the disposition of licenses granted pursuant to Paragraph 1, subdivision b.

Translation

m. Seventy-five per cent (75%) of the amount received from the disposition of licenses granted pursuant to Paragraph 1, subdivision c.

Commercial

n. Fifty per cent (50%) of the amount received from the disposition of licenses granted pursuant to Paragraph 1, subdivision d., provided that all expenses in connection therewith shall be borne by the Publisher.

Share to Other Authors

o. If any license granted by the Publisher pursuant to Paragraph 1 shall include material of others, the amount payable to the Author shall be inclusive of royalty to other authors.

Performance Rights

11. The Author appoints the Publisher as his exclusive agent to dispose of the performance rights including dramatic, musical, radio, television, motion picture and allied rights, subject to the Author's consent, and the Publisher shall receive a commission of ten per cent (10%) of the amount received.

In the event of the disposition of performance rights, the Publisher may grant to the purchaser the privilege to publish excerpts and summaries of the work in the aggregate not to exceed 7,500 words, for advertising and exploiting such rights, provided, however, that such grant shall require the purchaser to take all steps which may be necessary to protect the copyright of the work.

Rights Retained by Author

12. The Author agrees to notify the Publisher promptly of the disposition of any right which the Author has retained for himself.

Reports and Payments

13. The Publisher shall render semi-annual statements of account to the first day of April and the first day of October, and shall mail such statements during the July and January following, together with checks in payment of the amounts due thereon.

Should the Author receive an overpayment of royalty arising from copies reported sold but subsequently returned, the Publisher may deduct such overpayment from any further sums due the Author.

Upon his written request, the Author may examine or cause to be examined through certified public accountants the books of account of the Publisher in so far as they relate to the sale or licensing of the work.

Notwithstanding anything to the contrary in this or any prior agreement between the parties, the Author shall in no event be entitled to receive under this and all prior agreements with the Publisher more than $———— during any one calendar year. If in any one calendar year the total of the sums accruing to the Author under this and all prior agreements with the Publisher shall exceed such amount, he shall be entitled to receive the excess amount in any succeeding calendar year in which the sums accruing to him under this and all prior agreements with the Publisher do not exceed the maximum herein stated, provided that the total amount to which the Author may be entitled under this and all prior agreements with the Publisher in any succeeding calendar year shall not exceed the maximum herein stated.

Option for Next Work

14. The Author agrees to submit to the Publisher his next book-length work before submitting the same to any other publisher. The Publisher shall be entitled to a period of six weeks after the submission of the completed manuscript, which period shall not commence to run prior to one month after the publication of the work covered by this agreement, within which to notify the Author of its decision. If within that time the Publisher shall notify the Author of its desire to publish the manuscript, it shall thereupon negotiate with him with respect to the terms of such publication. If within thirty (30) days thereafter the parties are unable in good faith to arrive at a mutually satisfactory agreement for such publication, the Author shall be free to submit his manuscript elsewhere, provided, however, that he shall not enter into a contract for the publication of such manuscript with any other publisher upon terms less favorable than those offered by the Publisher.

Copies to Author

15. On publication the Publisher shall give ten (10) free copies to the Author, who may purchase further copies for personal use at a discount of forty per cent (40%) from the retail price.

Discontinuance of Publication

16. If the Publisher fails to keep the work in print and the Author makes written demand to reprint it, the Publisher shall, within sixty (60) days after the receipt of such demand, notify the Author in writing if it intends to comply. Within six (6) months thereafter, the Publisher shall reprint the work unless prevented from doing so by circumstances beyond its control. If the Publisher fails to notify the Author within sixty (60) days that it intends to comply, or, within six (6) months after such notification, the Publisher declines or neglects to reprint the work, then this agreement shall terminate and all

rights granted hereunder except those deriving from the option in Paragraph 14 shall revert to the Author, subject to licenses previously granted, provided the Author is not indebted to the Publisher for any sum owing to it under this agreement. After such reversion, the Publisher shall continue to participate to the extent set forth in this agreement in moneys received from any license previously granted by it. Upon such termination, the Author shall have the right for thirty (30) days thereafter to purchase the plates, if any, at one-fourth of the cost (including type setting).

If the work is under contract for publication or on sale in any edition in the United States, it shall be considered to be in print. A work shall not be deemed in print by reason of a license granted by the Publisher for the reproduction of single copies of the work. If the Publisher should determine that there is not sufficient sale for the work to enable it to continue its publication and sale profitably, the Publisher may dispose of the copies remaining on hand as it deems best, subject to the royalty provisions of Paragraph 10. In such event, the Author shall have the right, within two (2) weeks of the forwarding of a written notice from the Publisher, to a single purchase of copies at the "remainder" price.

Author's Property

17. Except for loss or damage due to its own negligence, the Publisher shall not be responsible for loss of or damage to any property of the Author.

Return of Manuscript

18. In the absence of written request from the Author prior to publication for their return, the Publisher, after publication of the work, may dispose of the original manuscript and proofs.

Suits for Infringement of Copyright

19. If the copyright of the work is infringed, and if the parties proceed jointly, the expenses and recoveries, if any, shall be shared equally, and if they do not proceed jointly, either party shall have the right to prosecute such action, and such party shall bear the expenses thereof, and any recoveries shall belong to such party; and if such party shall not hold the record title of the copyright, the other party hereby consents that the action be brought in his or its name.

Bankruptcy and Liquidation

20. If (a) a petition in bankruptcy is filed by the Publisher, or (b) a petition in bankruptcy is filed against the Publisher and such petition is finally sustained, or (c) a petition for arrangement is filed

by the Publisher or a petition for reorganization is filed by or against the Publisher, and an order is entered directing the liquidation of the Publisher as in bankruptcy, or (d) the Publisher makes an assignment for the benefit of creditors, or (e) the Publisher liquidates its business for any cause whatever, the Author may terminate this agreement by written notice and thereupon all rights granted by him hereunder shall revert to him. Upon such termination, the Author, at his option, may purchase the plates as provided in Paragraph 16 and the remaining copies at one-half of the manufacturing cost, exclusive of overhead. If he fails to exercise such option within sixty (60) days after the happening of any one of the events above referred to, the Trustee, Receiver, or Assignee may destroy the plates and sell the copies remaining on hand, subject to the royalty provisions of Paragraph 10.

Sums Due and Owing

21. Any sums due and owing from the Author to the Publisher, whether or not arising out of this agreement, may be deducted from any sum due or to become due from the Publisher to the Author pursuant to this agreement. For the purposes of this Paragraph a non-repayable unearned advance made to the Author pursuant to another agreement shall not be construed as being a sum due and owing, unless the Author is in default under such other agreement.

Law Applicable

22. This agreement shall be interpreted according to the law of the State of New York.

Assignment

23. This agreement shall be binding upon the heirs, executors, administrators and assigns of the Author, and upon the successors and assigns of the Publisher, but no assignment shall be binding on either of the parties without the written consent of the other.

Complete Agreement and Modification

24. This agreement constitutes the complete understanding of the parties. No modification or waiver of any provision shall be valid unless in writing and signed by both parties.

IN WITNESS WHEREOF the parties have duly executed this agreement the day and year first above written.

In the presence of

.... By ....
The Publisher

In the presence of

....
The Author

GLOSSARY OF INDUSTRY TERMS

ABOVE-THE-LINE—Generally the artistic elements in a show budget, e.g., actors and writers.

ACT—A vague term for theatrical material, suggestive of club dates and concert tours; occasionally useful in acquiring outright ownership of material not originally designed for a particular medium.

ADVANCE—An agreed fraction of compensation that may otherwise become due, paid before the due date and generally non-returnable, but later set off as a prepaid credit against incoming royalties or other compensation.

ALLIED RIGHTS—A motion-picture term for subsidiary rights (q.v.) but having a more fixed meaning in describing those rights that traditionally go with film rights, such as the right to exhibit a motion picture on television.

ASSIGNMENT—The transfer of basic ownership of certain rights such as copyright even though limited rights, e.g., in a particular medium, may be reserved by the original owner.

BELOW-THE-LINE—Generally the technical elements in a production budget, e.g., camera crews.

BILLING CREDIT—The display of one's name in connection with a dramatic or literary work.

BOILER-PLATE—Standard form provisions in a contract, frequently negotiable.

CAST ALBUM—The phonograph recording of a play, usually done by the original cast at a separate session, unlike the sound track album sometimes extracted from a film after the troupe disbands.

CONCERT TOUR—Successive bookings of an act or show other than at original fixed location.

COPYRIGHT—A right to prevent substantial copying. Considered by some to be a natural right of authors and by others a limited grant from the government.

CROSS-COLLATERALIZATION—Carrying over the losses or gains of one arrangement to another in some previously agreed form.

CROSS-INDEMNITY—The User's reciprocal undertakings to the rights owner with respect to script and other material added by the User.

CUT-OFF RIGHTS—Termination rights available to the User at one or more stages.

DOCUMENTARY—A performance theoretically serving as reportage rather than entertainment.

DROIT MORAL—In French law, the author's right to prevent unauthorized script changes.

EXCLUSIVITY—Sole right of use, i.e., the assurance that nobody else will compete by exploitation of the same or similar rights.

FIRST CLASS PRODUCTION—Presentation of a play under circumstances—including location of theatre—sufficient to affect union and other business terms; formerly, Broadway and West End productions and a few "out of town" groups.

FIRST NEGOTIATION—The right of the buyer to negotiate for a predetermined period before rival offers may be considered; basically little more than a right to be listened to.

FIRST REFUSAL—The right to meet, within specified time limits, competing terms of a rival offer for literary property.

FORCE MAJEURE—Circumstances beyond one's control.

FRONT MONEY—Funds available by contract for expenditure before the use of other investors' funds is permitted.

GROSS RECEIPTS—Sums actually received at the box office or elsewhere less only minor deductions such as local taxes.

LIBEL AND SLANDER—Defamation meeting certain legal qualifications and therefore actionable at law.

LICENSE—Grant of the right to use literary property on some limited basis, similar to renting as against owning.

LIVE—Performance directly transmitted to an audience rather

than recorded for later exhibition, although televising on videotape has sometimes been considered a "live" right.

MAJORS—Certain major financier-distributor companies in the motion picture field.

MERCHANDISING—A subsidiary right in many production contracts enabling the User to sell toys, games and other replicas of the performers if these performers have been induced to grant such rights to their producer.

MERGER—A promise that literary or dramatic material may no longer be used in a particular medium without specified new material such as music and lyrics.

MOST FAVORED NATIONS—A clause very popular with agents and designed to protect them against their own clients by assuring that whatever terms they negotiate for clients will be no worse than the terms accepted by others in the same production or series.

NET PROFITS—A variously defined share in certain productions and other ventures computed and paid after elaborately specified costs have been recouped.

OBJECTIVE STANDARD—Artistic control over script based on its meeting prearranged conditions rather than at the whim of the artist; the very fact that a third party determines whether or not it does so is a great help to the producer.

OPTION—The right to decide whether or not to continue, under prearranged conditions, a specified transaction or project, such as production of a play.

OVERCALL—The contractual right to call on investors in a play for additional pro rata contributions.

PACKAGER—The producer or manager who engages and furnishes multiple elements, such as actors and writers, in a show; technically their employer. Agents and other representatives frequently consider themselves packagers for assembling the elements on a client's behalf.

PAY OR PLAY—The explicit right to pay off a performer, artist or rights owner without actually utilizing his services or work, so as to protect the User against a lawsuit based on loss of enhancement of reputation.

PILOT—A sample episode made for the purpose of selling a program series and usually but not always used as one episode in the series or separately later on.

PREPRODUCTION DEAL—Purchase of film rights in a play before its capitalization and presentation on the stage. Possibly involves some financing of the play itself.

PUBLIC DOMAIN—The non-copyright area inhabited by works that may be used without permission.

READING FEE—In broadcasting, payment for the privilege of being the first to read literary material, cf., First Negotiation. In publishing (occasional), payment for the privilege of having one's literary material read and reported on, usually by an agent.

REASONABLE APPROVAL—A concept frequently reflected in contracts with authors or directors whose artistic approval rights, if not circumscribed by the objective standard of "reasonableness," might leave a producer with no recourse whatsoever in arbitration or legal proceedings.

RECOUPMENT—Recovery of original costs from all or in some cases particularized sources.

REMAKE—A new production based on the same literary property as an earlier one.

REPLAY FEES—Additional compensation, like a fixed royalty, payable on re-use of a program.

RESIDUALS—Additional compensation, generally with reference to television writers, for successive broadcasts of their script material.

REVERSION—Recapture by the original owner, e.g., an author, of rights previously granted to someone else.

RIGHT OF PRIVACY—A variously defined right to prevent use of one's name or likeness for commercial purposes without written permission.

ROYALTIES—An author's compensation computed in relation to sales or other uses of his work, and payable on the basis of a percentage or in fixed amounts.

RUN—The total composite of show exhibitions in a particular engagement or over a predefined number of stations. Re-runs in broadcasting are additional runs.

SALE—Technically an assignment (q.v.) for consideration but

used frequently to describe transfer of lesser rights; in those circumstances, more appropriately called a license, option or whatever fits.

SEQUEL—A new production related to an earlier one by the use of common elements such as characters; a kind of spin-off (q.v.) limited to one more show rather than a series.

SPECIAL—A television program which is not an episode in a series but a one-time show, usually presented with considerable fanfare.

SPIN-OFF—The extraction of one or more elements composing a complete work for separate use in a new and different work. The transplant of established characters to new stories.

STEP-DEAL—A series of consecutive options with prearranged cut-off rights designed to develop script material at the least possible risk.

SUBSIDIARIES—Rights other than the basic set of rights sought by a particular User, and therefore having no fixed meaning since film rights, for example, are subsidiary in a publishing contract but scarcely so in a motion picture contract.

SYNDICATION—Successive local uses of a program or printed material, e.g., non-network television sales.

TAKEOVER PROVISION—A right frequently granted networks to take over production of a show or series for specified reasons, such as the packager's bankruptcy.

TOP OF THE SHOW—The best terms given anyone doing the same function in a series, cf., Most Favored Nations.

TRADEMARKS—Brand names and other identifying symbols.

UNFAIR COMPETITION—A doctrine distinct from but not infrequently coupled with copyright, which is designed to protect against free-loading on another's work and other unfair practices.

Index